The Art of Orientation

The Art of Orientation

An Exploration of the Mosque through Objects

Edited and written by
Idries Trevathan, Mona AlJalhami, Murdo MacLeod, Mona Mansour

With contributions from
Abdullah H. Alkadi, Sami Angawi, Raeda Ashour, Lisa DeLong, Mohammed Abdel Bari, Oludamini Ogunnaike, Mohamed Abd el-Salam, Minwer al-Meheid

ithra
by aramco

HIRMER

Contents

Forewords

Foreword by Ithra's Director of Programs

In the Name of Allah, the Most Gracious, the Most Merciful

This exhibition *The Art of Orientation* represents a unique and ground-breaking event. This is the first major cooperation between a museum in Egypt and one in Saudi Arabia and represents a major step forward in cultural collaboration and strengthening of links between our two nations.

For over a millennium, Egypt, and Cairo in particular, has become a major center of the Islamic faith and culture in its own right. While the Two Holy Mosques of Makkah and Medina will always remain the heart of Islam, Cairo developed as a focus for learning and scholarship, as well as faith and practice. The sheer richness and variety of material on display in this exhibition, and this accompanying volume, bears witness to the vital role of Cairo in producing, preserving and studying Islamic art and heritage.

We are immensely indebted to the Supreme Council of Egyptian Antiquities, the Museum of Islamic Art in Cairo and the government of the Arab Republic of Egypt for their invaluable help and generosity in facilitating this exhibition, which brings together works of art from both the Cairene and Ithra collections and incorporates pieces from mosques across the world. So many people have worked so diligently to ensure that this exhibition has become a reality.

Our exhibition seeks to analyze and present the mosque, its function and purpose through a series of exhibits. We want to explore and understand what the various elements of the mosque do and how they interact in belief and worship. We also seek to explore the diverse functions of historic mosques in addition to worship.

The Art of Orientation is an exploration and tribute to the mosque, its origins, meanings and functions through a presentation of approximately 110 artifacts from across the Islamic world. We include a *minbar*, *mihrab* niches and calligraphy, as well as intricately produced prayer rugs, mosque lamps and Qur'anic manuscripts.

The exhibition also examines the evolution of mosque architecture from the humble mud-brick structure of the Prophet's (ﷺ) Mosque in Medina to the imposing stone structures of Cairo and Istanbul. However unlike previous expositions where the focus has been mostly on architectural aspects, this exhibition on mosques attempts to shed light on the meanings and contexts behind these buildings and their interiors. We seek to demonstrate how they served as both places of worship and meeting places where communities could meet and share ideas and knowledge, as well as practice charity and reflection.

In order to make the material accessible to a range of audiences, a fresh and contemporary approach is applied by weaving historical and contemporary narratives about objects displayed in the exhibition by leading Arab and international speakers (the contributing authors in this catalogue) including scholars, poets, artists, scientists and historians. These contemporary voices reflect on and shape stories that connect concepts, ideas and rituals to the objects while relating them to their origins and purposes.

At Ithra, we believe that we have a duty to make the exhibitions as meaningful and compelling as possible. To encourage the viewer to learn about, and experience, the historic evolution, function, aesthetics of mosques, high quality mosque models have been specially commissioned and virtual reality experiences of mosques from around the world are made available. The exhibition will also include other immersive techniques and experiences through the use of media and sound. Our desire is that our audiences get the maximum understanding of each and every item in this exhibition.

There is history, culture and creativity involved in the design and construction of everything we encounter in mosques. This is true of carpets, pulpits and lamps, as well as the buildings themselves. While function will dictate form, the designs also involve efforts to help believers in their worship and contemplation of the Almighty.

Part of Saudi Aramco's cultural commitment, the King Abdulaziz Center for World Culture, strives to enhance the lives of all Saudi citizens, while sparking creativity and innovation for a prosperous future for the Kingdom. I humbly trust that this exhibition will stimulate and illuminate our guests and audiences.

A truly prosperous, creative and sustainable future depends on fundamental understanding of where we have come from and which influences have created the world in which we live. We believe that this exhibition has the potential to deepen our understanding.

Naturally, this exhibition can only touch the surface of the vast creativity and artistic excellence found in mosques and their furnishings across the world. We can only hope that this small effort will spur some among our audiences to further study and analysis, as well as deeper contemplation.

Abdullah Al Rashid
Director of Programs
King Abdulaziz Center for World Culture

Foreword by Ithra's Head of Museums and Exhibits

In the Name of Allah, the Most Gracious, the Most Merciful

The Art of Orientation is a significant milestone both for the King Abdulaziz Center for World Culture and for the Kingdom of Saudi Arabia. We are deeply honored to be partnering with such a noteworthy institution as the Museum of Islamic Art in Cairo.

Words such as "unprecedented" and "iconic" risk being overused all too often in our current context. However the co-operation which has brought this exhibition to fruition is truly the first of its kind and is a substantial move in developing future collaboration among museums across the Middle East.

The Art of Orientation is a homage to the mosque and its various roles, as well as its context in both the Muslim and the wider community. We see in the exhibition the exploration of the mosque's evolution, aesthetics and functions spanning over 1,000 years across the world. It has served as far more than simply a structure for prayer and study of Scripture. From their inception, mosques were centers for administration, charity, discussion and culture. The architects, artists and artisans who worked on buildings, interiors and elements of the mosques strove to achieve ever greater functional, design and artistic heights.

The pursuit of artistic and creative greatness was not limited to monumental architecture and large-scale ornamentation, but encapsulated much smaller items such as prayer rugs, lamps and Qur'an stands. We observe this greatness in manuscripts and we even see it in administrative documents, with the use of spectacular and beautiful calligraphy to enhance their majesty.

We trust that our efforts will encourage those who visit the exhibition to explore further the sheer depth and variety of the functional splendor found in and around mosques across the world.

Laila Al-Faddagh
Head of Museums and Exhibits
King Abdulaziz Center for World Culture

Foreword by the Secretary General of the Supreme Council of Egyptian Antiquities

In the Name of Allah, the Most Gracious, the Most Merciful

Like the sun shedding its rays all over the world, from the east to the west, the great Islamic civilization became a beacon guiding humanity to the path of renaissance in science, art and knowledge.

A testament to this legacy is the rich history spanning several centuries and dynasties, and the admired monuments and artifacts reflecting breathtaking Islamic architecture and art: creativity which has attracted the attention of the entire world.

Undoubtedly, meetings of civilizations are considered defining turning points in human history. They did, and still can, disperse darkness and pave the way for the light of knowledge to shine everywhere.

Islamic civilization has played a significant role in this interaction between civilizations. Its seminal influence has been continuous through the ages regardless of the location.

Throughout their long history, Egypt and Hijaz have been linked by historical, economic, political and cultural ties. Hijaz was the focal point for rulers of the entire Islamic world, which comes as no surprise since it is the cradle of Islam. Also, being home to Islamic Holy Sites, Hijaz became a unique region and a destination for pilgrims and visitors.

The Impact of these deeply-rooted ties has been seen in on the social level, such as intermarriage between citizens of the two nations; the similarities in both their dialects and other social traditions. In this regard, we cannot help but mention the main factors that contributed to deepening the relations between the two countries; namely the annual pilgrimage caravan from Egypt to Hijaz, also known as the "Egyptian Mahmal".

Art has long been considered an eyewitness and a true mirror that clearly reflects an expressive image of the advances and cultural progress of nations. It also seeks to lay the foundations for the desired cultural dialogue between peoples.

Islamic art is an international art which has left its mark in history. As an all-encompassing art, it influenced many aspects of life, including science, medicine, astronomy, chemistry and engineering, while also being creative and descriptive of beauty wherever it may be found.

Those who contemplate Islamic art will become, at first glance, certain of its unique qualities, which have had a clear impact on the whole world. Muslim artists were able to combine elements, which Islamic art drew from other art forms during its early years, with other external factors to create a rich and independent identity for Islamic art.

From the beginning, Muslim artists devoted most of their interest to the mosque, due to the influential role it plays in Islamic society as the house of Allah the Almighty. The mosque was also a place of unity for the Islamic nation, a center where Muslims converge not only to pray, but to exchange views, discuss life issues, and embark on the right path, on which the identity of both individuals and nations is built. Mosques represented the melting pot where all members of society unite, and all differences dissolve.

As such, art became an important factor in shaping the identity of the mosque, and an integral part of its heritage and development. Encouraged by Muslim sultans and princes, architects and artists competed to build and decorate every single part of the mosque.

Several masterpieces played a functional role within mosques, and have thus long been associated with them, such as *minbars*, *mihrabs* and Qur'an stands, in addition to lighting tools such as *mishkahs*, chandeliers, lamps, candlesticks, and other artifacts of different shapes and patterns. All these masterpieces reflected the ability of Muslim artists to innovate across different eras and locations.

Represented by the Ministry of Tourism and Antiquities, Egypt believes in the key role museums play in the lives of societies, and the importance of mutual cooperation to achieve their mission, while embracing the idea of cultural exchange between Arab countries. One especially important goal is reviving the glory of Islamic civilization by unveiling the most important artifacts through international exhibitions such as this exhibition, *The Art of Orientation*, which sheds light on masterpieces of Islamic art which have been associated with mosques, and in turn reflect the progress and prosperity of Islamic civilization and arts.

Dr. Mostafa Waziri
Secretary General of the Supreme Council of Egyptian Antiquities
Ministry of Tourism and Antiquities
Arab Republic of Egypt

Foreword by the Director of the Museum of Islamic Art in Cairo

In the Name of Allah, the Most Gracious, the Most Merciful

This exhibition is of considerable significance. Throughout the history of Islam, the mosque has been a central feature of life and has helped give direction to the faithful. We are also privileged to be part of this new sphere of Egyptian-Saudi cooperation in the fields of Islamic culture and arts. We at the Museum of Islamic Art in Cairo are proud to participate in this exhibition by displaying 84 Islamic masterpieces and priceless objects, of various materials and functions, for a period of two years at Ithra Museum at the King Abdulaziz Center for World Culture.

The concept of the exhibition reflects the role of the mosque in the artistic and civil life of Muslims throughout their history. The display narrative seeks to highlight the value of the mosque, the extent of the mosque's contribution to building the Muslim community, and how mosques have addressed the most important religious, political, social, cultural and intellectual issues.

I am delighted to express my thanks and appreciation to all my colleagues at the Museum of Islamic Art in Cairo and at Ithra Museum in the King Abdulaziz Center for World Culture, who spent their time and effort in order to realize this compelling exhibition. I sincerely hope that this exhibition will prove a model to cultural institutions in Egypt and the Kingdom of Saudi Arabia regarding the preservation of Islamic civilizational heritage, and presenting the Islamic arts to our audiences.

Dr. Mamdouh Osman
Director
The Museum of Islamic Art in Cairo

Curatorial Statement

An Exhibition on the Mosque

People everywhere go to museums not only to gaze at beautiful and unique objects from the past, but also to find answers to today's questions. Our own research here in Saudi Arabia has shown that our audiences want the presentation of Islamic art to help them explore questions about identity and belonging.

Visitors expect modern museums to present the specific contexts of objects and their connections between the present and the past, as well as their geography, history, culture and the societies from which they originate. This desire to learn more also embraces the psychological, aesthetic and even religious aspects of objects. A broader and more complete interpretation appeals to modern Saudi audiences and meets the need to treat Islamic visual culture as a living tradition that continues to shape identity.

Interestingly the results of the research contrast with general museum practices that tend to focus exclusively on the objects, their provenance and their physical condition. Questions of meaning and context normally do not feature in museum displays. Generally, works of Islamic art and architecture, whether presented in books or exhibitions, are treated as autonomous works of art, without mention of historical events or culture, or indeed, even the people involved: patrons, artists, architects or craftsmen. There is no sense of the human element around such objects nor of what they may have represented, their function and meanings within the societies that owned and used them.

Audience research shows a strong desire among the public to learn about the art, architecture and functions of mosques from around the world, with a particular focus on the Two Holy Mosques of Makkah and Medina. Focus groups indicated significant interest in aspects of Islamic civilization directly connected to the mosque theme, including the economic – to zakat (alms) and *waqf* (charitable endowments) – and the teaching of religious sciences. The subject of mosques seemed to have been overlooked by museums, both regionally and internationally, and as a result, many people know little about their rich cultural and social history. In the view of the great art historian Oleg Grabar, the wider contribution of mosques is almost always neglected: "the historian often tends to forget people ... The worshippers are absent from the holy places as presented by the historian; and the changing needs of a dynamic culture are hardly matters of great importance [for the historian]." (Grabar. 2002, 245)

The exhibition which this book accompanies endeavors to address these gaps and challenges. Indeed, as a public institution, the museum at the King Abdulaziz Center for World Culture (Ithra) has a responsibility to respond. The question is, how precisely to achieve this?

Addressing social and cultural contexts of Islamic art requires completely rethinking the museum presentation of Islamic art objects. What stories ought to be told and what approaches should be applied in their telling? How does one address the physical size and scale of a mosque in an exhibition, let alone capture the wonder and majesty? How do exhibitions recreate the all-embracing, rich, subtle weave of decorative patterns and textures that make mosques like Suleymaniye in Istanbul or Makkah's Grand Mosque so mesmerizing? Then there is the question of context; neither the decorative arts nor the furniture that were incorporated into mosque spaces were intended for display in an art gallery. Such objects were not understood as self-referential works of art or "masterpieces" but were seen and experienced collectively in specific settings and in rituals that framed their significance. Therefore, the use and meaning of these objects are dependent on their original contexts and architectural settings.

To address some of these challenges, *The Art of Orientation* tells the story of the mosque in a new way. Responding to visitor interest that focuses on the cultural context of the mosque, this book endeavors to examine the complex interplay of theological, sociological, economic and artistic factors by looking at objects that that have been housed and used in such buildings. We include a wide range of items, from architectural ornament such as calligraphic and arabesque tiles, to mosque furniture including lamps, prayer rugs, Qur'an stands and manuscripts. Through these we can glimpse the breadth, complexity and multifaceted nature of these mosques, and how they have graced history.

The interpretation of these objects is also approached in a novel way by infusing the human element back into our understanding of them. Ten guests have been invited to participate in shaping stories around specially selected "gateway" objects that bring alive contexts and people. Each one connects to a web of other related objects, which were selected for their aesthetic quality and richly documented histories. Alongside these objects, historical architectural pieces, archival photography and images, and video documentation of Islamic architecture anchor the visitor to the place and period of each story. These visual aids provide further context for the utilitarian objects, including lamps and carpets, which are on display.

To provide new and fresh perspectives, we selected a broad range of contributors – not only art historians and curators, but also architects, philosophers, artists, poets and religious scholars. Some contributors were chosen for their in-depth knowledge about a particular type of object or theme, others simply for their elegant and thought-provoking insight into more general aspects of premodern Islamic culture. What they all had in common was the consistently high quality of their work within their respective fields. Another shared trait was their willingness to engage with different ways of addressing the multifaceted nature of the mosque through objects. We asked them to present the object in ways they felt worked best for them. The contributors readily met our challenge, applying a variety of approaches to their topics. The result is, as hoped, a more insightful and expanded understanding of the mosque.

Introduction

Mosque, Art and Orientation

> Verily, We have seen the turning of your (Mohammed's ﷺ) face towards the heaven. Surely, We shall turn you to the qiblah (prayer direction) that shall please you, so turn your face in the direction of the Masjid al-Haram (the Sanctuary in Makkah). And wheresoever you people are, turn your faces (in prayer) in that direction.
> (Holy Qur'an, Surah Al-Bakarah, verse 144)

On receiving these verses of the Holy Qur'an, Prophet Mohammed (ﷺ), turned his congregation in prayer southward to Makkah instead of, as previously, north towards Jerusalem. The mosque on the outskirts of Medina where this event occurred, subsequently known as the Mosque of the Two Qiblas (Masjid al-Qiblatayn), serves as a reminder of this momentous event when, in the year 624 (second year after Hijra), the focus of Muslim devotion was turned towards Makkah and thus Islam was thus given an axis and orientation of its own. As the desert Arabs fanned outwards from the Arabian Peninsula bringing Islam westward to the shores of the Iberian Peninsula and eastward to the borders of China, mosques were built, forming a massive concentric wheel with the spokes converging on a single point in Makkah: the Ka'ba.

In simple terms, a mosque can be thought of as a building erected around this horizontal axis, of the qibla (direction of the Ka'ba), and, as such, a mosque is no more than a wall at right angles to the qibla axis. However, at its most basic definition, a mosque is simply a "place of prostration" as described in the Holy Qur'an. Indeed the Prophet Mohammed (ﷺ) was known to have said that, with the exception of a few places, the whole earth was created as clean and pure (*tahur*), and as a place of worship, or a mosque (*masjid*), to him and his followers (al-Tirmidhi and Sahih Muslim). Hence, a mosque can be any place or structure as long as its axis is correctly orientated towards Makkah.

Place, space and time

Since the orientation of prayer in the mosque was not simply a matter of traditional practice but was a command from God to the Prophet Mohammed (ﷺ), establishing the correct physical orientation, in addition to finding the correct time of prayer, has always been of supreme importance and there exists a long and established literary and scientific tradition in the Muslim world devoted to its study. In our wide-ranging Chapter 1, which uses a 13th-century astrolabe as its focus, Abdullah Alkadi examines the broader significance of this tradition in relation to his own research on conceptions of time and space. In particular, he links the functions of astrolabe in measuring time and space in relation his groundbreaking investigations in tracing the major travel routes taken by Prophet Mohammed (ﷺ) and his companions using modern scientific methods such as the Global Positioning System (GPS). While the traditional methods for navigating journeys, finding the qibla or calculating the prayer times have been supplanted by modern digital instruments controlled by satellite, this Islamic tradition continues to be of central importance both in relation to Islamic religion, and the function and significance of the mosque.

Establishing the qibla and the prayer times was also of primary concern for Muslims who traveled great distances, including those pilgrims en route to Makkah. The pilgrimage, or Hajj, occurs once a year during the month of Dhu al-Hijjah, and elaborate rites on this occasion include visits to the Ka'ba in the Masjid al-Haram (Grand Mosque of Makkah), which is often depicted on certificates and mementos the pilgrims acquired. In Chapter 4, Raeda Ashour, an artist who takes inspiration from these manuscripts in creating contemporary depictions of the *Haramayn* (Two Holy Mosques), investigates a notable example comprising a 17th-century tile depicting the Grand Mosque in Makkah. This tile presents a topographical rendering of the *haram* (sanctuary) showing details including various holy structures, gates, minarets and such. Depictions of this kind generally present the sanctuary which is carefully labelled and the space around the diagram often contains the verse from the Holy Qur'an (Surah Al-Imran: 97) which enjoins the performance of Hajj on all Muslims who can afford it. When one considers that vast majority of Muslims lacked the means to travel to Makkah and perform Hajj, the powerful emotional impact of this image upon devout Muslims would have been significant. Before the advent of photography, seeing the Ka'ba depicted in a manuscript or tile could evoke a profound response in viewers since the qibla represents the focus towards which Muslims have directed their devotion throughout their lives.

Mosque as community center

The notion of directional orientation, or qibla, can be understood to work on at least two levels; ritually as the focus of prayer and socially as a focal point which the entire community (*ummah*) can direct their attention. Both the ritual and social levels are fulfilled within the mosque. Indeed, these structures represent the heart of Muslim life and reflect the attachment and commitment to the ideals of Islamic religion.

The foremost authority on the history of the Two Holy Mosques, Sami Angawi, explains in Chapter 2 that, in addition to worship, the mosque was also a place of great social and cultural importance. From the beginning, the mosque was at once the religious and social center of the Islamic community, as well as a center for learning and social welfare. In order to understand the mosque in the crucial early stages of its development, Angawi writes that it is necessary to point to its role as community center and as the house of the Prophet Mohammed (ﷺ). Here, worship was conducted, youth educated, the sick and poor were cared for, public announcements made, ambassadors lodged, meetings held, parades reviewed and cases tried, the treasury housed and the councils assembled. Thus, it began as a community center of a new faith where religious and worldly life were pursued simultaneously. This formative period of early Islamic society within the Prophet's (ﷺ) Mosque in Medina formed the prototype to which all subsequent mosques adhered, in terms of architecture and functions.

While the development of specifically Islamic institutions later removed from the mosque the functions which it had during the time of the Prophet (ﷺ), some of these lingered well into the premodern age. In fact, sometimes the auxiliary functions were expanded, with multiple appendages to the mosque. Thus, in an effort to model the Prophet's house, early mosques continued to serve as town halls, as well as other facilities not directly connected to worship. Many large Friday (*Jami*) mosques testify to this versatile nature and almost never stand alone; they stand amidst an entire complex and are reached by passing through libraries, gardens and past lines of low regular buildings dedicated to schools, soup kitchens, to almshouses, to hostelries and to other supplementary services offered by the mosque. A good example of this can be found in the 16th-century Suleymaniye Mosque in Istanbul which was built in association with a wide range of buildings that helped the community, including caravanserais, mausolea, ribats, madrasas, theological colleges and soup kitchens. Therefore, while the specialization of the mosque in the modern age has shed many of its earlier functions, historically speaking, to found a mosque was not simply to set up a new place of worship, it was to establish a building that brought new life to an entire section of an urban environment.

The money used to construct and maintain mosques like the Suleymaniye was not paid for from taxes but from charitable donations through a unique Islamic foundation called *waqf*. To understand the origins of the *waqf*, it is necessary to cite the following Hadith (Sahih Muslim) which contains a statement by the Prophet (ﷺ) regarding posterity: "When a person dies, his achievements expire, except with regard to three things – ongoing charity or knowledge from which people benefit or a son who prays for him." (Trans. Singer. 2002, 5). Therefore, "ongoing charity" – literally an endowment, or *waqf* – allows an individual's pious works to continue especially through the financial support of a mosque institution. In Chapter 3, through her study of an 18th-century Ottoman firman which assigns the responsibilities of Beshir Agha as chief inspector of the *waqf* to the Prophet's (ﷺ) Mosque in Medina, curator Mona AlJalhami demonstrates how the *waqf* foundations became an important and widespread legal strategy that provided big cities like Madina, Makkah, Cairo and Istanbul with hundreds of mosque institutions built and financially supported by perpetual endowments.

Education and knowledge

Because education was held in such high esteem in the Islamic world, *waqf* money was given generously to mosque institutions and learning prospered in the main cities of the Islamic world. Finances covered the teachers' salaries, accommodation, and food for the students and scholarships for those in need. Ibn Battuta (d. 1377), the famous 14th-century Muslim traveler, talks about the student who was supported 100 percent: "Anyone who wishes to pursue a course of studies or to devote himself to the religious life receives every aid to the execution of this purpose." During the first few centuries of Islam, almost all schooling took place in the mosque, where teachers of particular subjects would address large gatherings of students who came from far and wide. A teacher would sit on the floor of the mosque, leaning against a column, or on raised seat, or sometimes even on the *minbar* (pulpit), with his pupils grouped in a circle around him. It is still a common sight in many mosques around the world to see these study circles called *Halaqat al-Ilm* or *halaqa* gathered around a professor or the imam seated on a high chair to make him visible and audible to the students.

By the 11th century, however, separate institutions of higher education were established in the major cities. These buildings were almost always associated with, or physically connected to, the city's main Friday mosque. This type of institution known as the madrasa (literally a place of study) provided space for teaching and prayers, as well as student and faculty accommodation, and was often sponsored by the *waqf* institution. For example, the powerful Seljuk vizier Nizam al-Mulk (d. 1092) founded madrasas known as *nizamiyyas* in all major cities in the Seljuk realms, including the famous al-Nizamiyya of Baghdad, where the famous theologian al-Ghazali (d. 1111) was known to have taught. Some mosques are the oldest functioning universities in the world today, such as the Zaytuna Mosque in Tunis and the Al-Azhar in Cairo, which were established in 863 and 970 respectively. The latter, Al-Azhar, was the focal point of higher learning during the Fatimid period and its reputation attracted the greatest intellects of the age, including Ibn al-Haytham (d. 1040) and Ibn al Khaldun (d. 1406). Another grand college mosque complex was al-Qarawiyyin in Fez, Morocco, which was built as a mosque in 859 by a devout woman called Fatima al-Fihri (d. 880) and developed into a center for religious instruction, gradually extending its education to other subjects such as astronomy, geography and medicine, theology, law, rhetoric, prose, logic, arithmetic, grammar and chemistry. Likewise, Islamic learning also flourished on the periphery of the Muslim world deep in sub-Saharan Africa at the University of Sankore, in Timbuktu, which developed out of the Sankore Mosque, founded in 989.

To support scholarly pursuit and learning, particularly within the religious sciences, many large mosques housed public book collections. In fact, from the early centuries of Islam, it was impossible to find a mosque, the place of learning, without a collection of books. Mosque libraries were commonly called *Dar al-Kutub*, or the house of books, and they were the focus of intellectual activity. The grand Umayyad Mosque in Aleppo, Syria, probably had the oldest mosque library, called the *Sayfiya*, which housed a collection of 10,000 volumes, whereas the Zaytuna Mosque in Tunis reportedly had a collection in excess of 100,000 volumes. As Idries Trevathan explains by way of an early 19th-century wooden Holy Qur'an writing tablet (*luwh*) from Morocco in Chapter 5, education was not just restricted to the bookish but extended to more vocational training including calligraphy. Indeed, mosques employed calligraphers to teach their students the art of beautiful writing and many of these students went on to produce books for the library, including beautiful copies of manuscripts of the Holy Qur'an which were often prominently displayed within the prayer halls on a folding stand, or *rahil*, during the holy month of Ramadan.

Beauty and function

Monumental Qur'anic script is also one of the hallmarks of mosque architecture and was applied to wide variety of media, from carved inscriptions in wood and stone to painted and glazed ceramic tiles. Out of various styles of script, two in particular – solid, monumental Kufic and elegant Thulth – were the most commonly employed in mosque architecture. The display of the Holy Qur'an, or any part thereof, on the surfaces of the mosque provides the viewer with a message of focus and contemplation. Such inscriptions were often suitably selected for their locations in which they were displayed, as for example in verse (35:41): "Verily, Allah grasps the heavens and the earth lest they should move away from their places" which are often seen prominently displayed on the inside of mosque domes, or the "Light Verse" (24:35): "Allah is the Light of the heavens and the earth" incorporated in the stained-glass windows and other light features within the prayer hall.

Different types of abstract pattern were used to complement the inscriptions, comprising vegetal and floral ornament, sometimes known as "arabesque" or geometrical forms such as stars, derived from shapes such as circles, squares, triangles and polygons. Spread over vast surfaces in the mosques, this ornamentation provided a perfect setting for the word of the Holy Qur'an. In her expert analysis of a 14th-century Seljuk star and cross ceramic tile panel in Chapter 6, the geometer Lisa Delong advocates the idea that such patterns are not superficial embellishment but instead reflect a belief in an underlying order. From her perspective, Islamic patterns not only reflect particular ideas, but can actually qualitatively transform the ambience of a mosque. Together with monumental calligraphy, it is an art form that perfectly complements the mosque, whose finest works simultaneously appeal to the devotional, intellectual and aesthetic sensibilities of the onlooker. The most refined expressions of Islamic patterns transform the walls of the mosque into a powerful focus of serene contemplation.

Objects of orientation

The objects and furniture within mosques always combine beauty with function and among the best examples of this union is the mosque lamp, particularly those that date to Mamluk Cairo. One significant example which is attributed to the 14th-century Sultan al-Nasir Muhammad ibn Qalawun Mosque is discussed beautifully by the poet Mohammed Abdel Bari in Chapter 7. Before electric lighting became common in mosques during the early 20th century, these lamps – which for larger mosques numbered into their hundreds – were lit manually and required teams of people to light them before evening or early morning prayers. Many mosques still retain detailed *waqf* records dating back hundreds of years that specify the payments to the light keepers who maintained the lamps by replacing the wicks, cleaning the glass and replacing the dirty water, as well as refilling their oil.

The qibla not only affected the alignment of the mosque, it also had an enormous bearing on the beauty and design of objects, furniture and architectural elements. The most obvious example is found in the *mihrab*, which is an empty niche placed within the main wall at the front of the mosque's prayer hall. From its placement, the *mihrab* indicates the direction of the qibla, as well as defining the spot where the imam would lead congregational prayers. In his study of a 12th-century portable wooden *mihrab* from Cairo, the Harvard-trained scholar Oludamini Ogunnaike presents in Chapter 8 the broad nexus of associations and meanings related to the *mihrab* niche throughout Islamic history.

In addition to the *mihrab*, another feature in the mosque that indicated the direction of the qibla is the prayer rug or *sejjadah* (literally place of prostration). These prayer rugs, either single or multiple row "saf" carpets, would often reflect the splendor of the mosque's interior. For example, in the art historian and curator Mohamed Ahmed Abd el-Salam's study of a beautiful 16th-century Ottoman prayer rug in Chapter 9, which originally formed part of the central upper tier of a communal multiple prayer rug in the Selimiye Mosque in Edirne, Turkey, we find fascinating correlations between motifs and designs in the carpet and those features that are present in the architecture of the mosque such as the *mihrab* and mosque lamp.

To the right of the *mihrab* niche stands the *minbar*, or pulpit, which is the elevated stepped seat from where the imam delivers the Friday sermon, and where, historically, Muslim rulers (caliphs), as well as provincial governors or their representatives, made important public announcements. In Chapter 10, the scholar Minwer al-Meheid provides an expert reading of a beautiful 18th-century wooden Berber *minbar* which is believed to have originated from a small congregational mosque in Morocco's Atlas Mountains. In addition to providing the broader context surrounding the history and use of the *minbar*, Meheid shares how he came to manage the painstaking reconstruction of the famous 12th-century *minbar* of Saladin following a disastrous fire at Jerusalem's Al-Aqsa Mosque in 1969. Like the buildings in which they were housed, these *minbars* – which are considered among the greatest masterpieces of Islamic art – were ultimately modeled on the original Prophet's *minbar*, which remained in his mosque for around 600 years, only succumbing to a fire in the 13th century. During this time, the pulpit was a reminder of the blessed presence of the Prophet (ﷺ) and many visitors and travelers wrote moving accounts of it. One of earliest was by a companion of the Prophet (ﷺ), the famous Arab poet Hassan Ibn Thabit who wrote (Trans. Stetkevych, 61):

> At Taybah [Medina] there remain the Prophet's
> relics and a luminous
> Encounter place, while other relics fade
> And waste away.
> Indelible are the signs of that inviolate abode,
> Where the Guide's pulpit stands on which he used to mount.
> It stands so clear, the contours firm – and there
> His precinct with a prayer-place and a mosque.
> There his chambers are, there
> The Lord's light found its repose,
> To give him light and warmth –
> Signs which will not be effaced as time goes by,

Finding renewal in each decay.
I recognized the Prophet's traces
And where I saw him last,
A grave in whose dust he, hidden, lies.

Final words

The inspiration, model and example laid down by the Prophet Mohammed (ﷺ) and his companions within the context of the mosque is perhaps the most pervasive and reoccurring theme that runs through the course of this book. It was within the confines of the Masjid Al Nabawi (the mosque of the Prophet [ﷺ]), during the seventh century, where the blueprint for all later Muslim places of worship was established, and also where the tone was set for Muslim community structure.

The following chapters see ten scholars from across the globe, particularly the Arab world, address works representing various aspects of the mosque, including lamps, prayer rugs, a *minbar* and *mihrab*. Through their stories, it is hoped that the reader will learn to appreciate not only how such structures were built, but also how they functioned in relation to the society they served. Ultimately, the aim of this book and the exhibition it accompanies is to show how such buildings not only served the highest personal thought and commitment to God, but also how they facilitated everyday life, making it better for as many people as possible, in a very real and tangible way.

Chapters

1 The Astrolabe: Finding Place, Space and Time

Abdullah H. Alkadi

> And the sun runs on its fixed course for a term (appointed). That is the Decree of the All-Mighty, the All-Knowing. And the moon, We have measured for it mansions (to traverse) till it returns like the old, dried, curved date stalk. It is not for the sun to overtake the moon, nor does the night outstrip the day. They all float, each in an orbit. (Qur'an. Surah Ya-Sin, verses 38–40)

> Verily! In the creation of the heavens and the earth, and in the alternation of night and day, and the ships which sail through the sea with that which is of use to mankind, and the water (rain) which Allah sends down from the sky and makes the earth alive therewith after its death, and the moving (living) creatures of all kinds that He has scattered therein, and in the veering of winds and clouds which are held between the sky and the earth, are indeed Ayat (proofs, evidences, signs, etc.) for people of understanding. (Qur'an. Surah Al-Bakarah, verse 164)

These verses, and others like them, from the Holy Qur'an provided early Muslims with much inspiration in observing the heavens. Their description of celestial orbits and courses conveys a clear message that behind these phenomena lies a coherent system that humanity is invited to reflect upon and study. This, combined with the necessity for the Arabs to navigate the vast deserts with the help of stars, provided a powerful impetus to the study of astronomy from the beginning of Islamic era. Most importantly, however, tracking the stars was critical for determining the correct times of the five daily prayers, as well as calculating the orientation of prayer and mosques towards the Holy Ka'ba in Makkah (the qibla).

While fulfilling these requirements was not problematic for Muslims living in the immediate vicinity and areas around Makkah, as soon as Muslim communities spread to areas further away, in places like Africa and Central Asia, the orientation towards the qibla became much more

← Detail of 1.1, 1.2

difficult to determine. As a result, some mosques on the periphery of the Islamic world were not always precisely aligned with the qibla.

The astrolabe: function and application

Before scientific methods became available, the qibla was determined based on the practices of the early companions of the Prophet Mohammed (ﷺ) and his successors. However, as the Islamic realms expanded, spreading out across the globe from Spain to China, more scientifically accurate devices were needed to calculate the direction of Makkah. This challenge led to the development from the ninth century onwards of a unique Islamic geographical tradition. Maps were drawn and instruments developed which gave an accurate direction of prayer for a large number of locations.

The most important Islamic astronomical instrument developed during this early period was the planispheric astrolabe, as shown in Figure 1.1, which consists of a set of closely fitting circular parts made of cast silver. With knowledge of the longitude where one is located, this astrolabe can determine the exact direction of the qibla. Moreover, this astrolabe can be used to measure time in a very precise way, at day as well as at night, using the trajectory of the sun or the stars in the sky. This device was indispensable in establishing the schedule for prayer times. The astrolabe

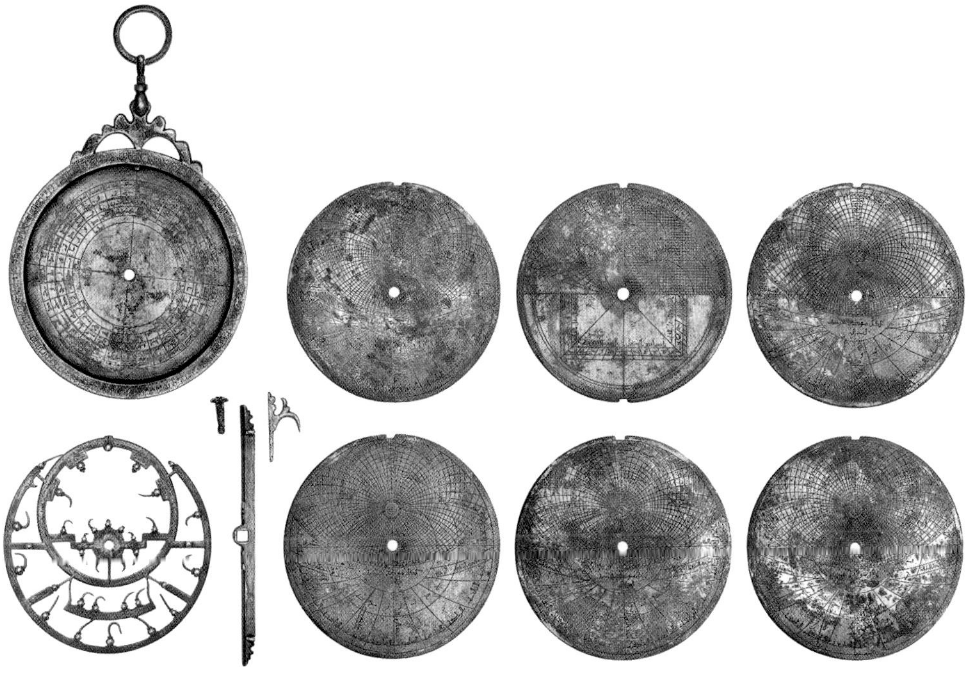

1.1, 1.2 **Astrolabe**
This silver astrolabe is signed by Muhammad Ibn Fattuh Al Khumairi, the most renowned astronomer of Islamic Spain. His astrolabes were copied by later astronomers both in the Islamic world and in Europe. Each of the accompanying plates is inscribed with major Spanish cities, including Seville, Cordoba and Toledo.

Seville, Spain, 1250
Engraved cast silver with gold pins
Diameter: 21.5 cm
Ithra Museum 2020.0069

was not restricted to religious use. When used with a number of other instruments, it could be applied to navigating both land and sea.

While this 13th-century Spanish-made astrolabe is quite small, designed to be portable and neatly fit in the hands, others were larger and could be up to a couple of meters in circumference. The main part of the astrolabe, called the mother (*umm* in Arabic) or *mater* in Latin, comprises a thick brass plate which has its center hollowed out to leave a raised outer rim on its edge. Within this hollowed out area sits a round plate containing a two-dimensional projection of the Earth's latitudinal lines. Over that plate, another circular feature called the "rete" contains the locations of certain well-known stars in the sky. On the reverse, a pivoting and rotatable device helps the altitude of a star to be determined – often the starting point of a calculation. On the outer rim of the *umm* are engraved the degrees from 0 to 360. However, instead of numbers, the astrolabe uses the abjad numbering system which assigns numerical values to the 28 letters of the Arabic alphabet. Since the geography of the sky changes with latitude, astrolabes commonly came with a series of plates for the different latitudes of large cities around the Islamic world. It was possible to swap the plates according to how far north or south the user was.

In the simplest terms, an astrolabe is a two-dimensional model of the heavens, showing how the sky looks at a specific place and time. Thus, astrolabes can be considered the astronomical computers of their time, solving problems relating to the position of planets, the sun, the stars and time. Time and place are brought together in a single device.

Tracking the Hijra through place and time

The notion of "place and time" (*Makan wa Zaman*) within the Muslim tradition is a topic I have devoted my life to examining. Over the last 25 years, I have focused on the geography of the Holy Qur'an and *Seera* (life of the Prophet Mohammed [ﷺ]) devoting countless hours and days, and traversing thousands of miles to trace the journeys taken by the Prophet (ﷺ) and his companions across the Arabian Peninsula and beyond. In the course of this study, I have conducted many field expeditions, collecting data, recording Global Positioning System (GPS) coordinates, identifying landmarks, calculating distances, and covering as much of these routes as possible by foot. Every available resource was consulted, from Hadith to

1.3 **The Hijra Route**
Prof. Abdullah Alkadi (left) and his companions traveling the Hijra route on foot.

Seera literature and narrations, to historical documents and maps. I have also conducted extensive interviews with local residents and guides to glean oral history about those locations.

However, one journey in particular, the Hijra, has been the consummation and focus of my life's work. The Hijra ("Migration" or "Flight") generally refers to Prophet Mohammed's (ﷺ) exodus with his closest companion, Abu Bakr (may God be pleased with him), from Makkah to Medina looking for freedom. My research into the route they took involved field expeditions, and utilized advanced GPS and GIS technology. More specifically, the coordinates along this route were recorded through cameras equipped with GPS, from which a complete geographical mapping of each event could be formed. Schematic and detailed area survey maps were produced for each site based on a number of satellite images from Google Earth, along with actual photographs taken from these sites. Prominent photographers joined me on many of these journeys including the award-winning British photographer Peter Sanders. As part of this project, I also checked this information against the narrations (*Riwayat*) by the biographers of the Prophet (ﷺ). I searched for and identified popular landmarks and cross-referenced them with the narrations. In tandem, I also carefully weighed the importance and accuracy of each narration.

One of the most important and interesting aspects in my search for the Hijra route was meeting and talking to the local people who were born and lived in the places along the way. Many of those whom I encountered were still leading traditional lives, unaffected by technology and modernization, and maintained a strong connection to their customs and history. I sought out the elders and recorded their knowledge and oral traditions that had been passed down to them about the Hijra. In doing so, I was able to ascertain the ancient names of the various landmarks, including valleys and mountains, and cross-check them with historical accounts.

Bringing together all this information, I was able to divide the journey into periods of time, hour by hour, day by day, through association with various landmarks and terrains. Through my painstaking research, I was able to correct and expand previous studies on the Hijra and provide the most accurate account, through visual reference, of this hugely significant journey. I am honored that the results of my research, as well as the particular methodology applied, is now taught in universities around Saudi Arabia.

The Hijra from Makkah to Medina in 622 can be examined from different perspectives, including its explicit and hidden meanings and significance. The Hijra is one of the most important events in the history of Islam and it is for this reason that Caliph Omar ibn Al Khattab (may God be pleased with him) adopted the Hijra date to begin measuring the passage of time. The Islamic (Hijri) calendar comprises 12 lunar months, the beginnings and endings of which are determined by the sighting of the crescent moon.

In fact, the Hijra's importance is not limited to Islamic history or to Muslims, but represents a moment which changed the whole of human history. It not only initiated the social and political reshaping of the Arabian Peninsula, but also had a transformational impact on the history of the world. When Prophet Mohammed (ﷺ) migrated from Makkah to Medina, he did not just relocate and take refuge in another city. In physical terms, while the Hijra was a journey between two cities about 450 km apart, its broader significance marks the beginning of an era, a civilization, a culture and a history for the whole of humanity.

GPS versus the astrolabe

Today, the use of the GPS is widespread and accessible. But decades ago, when I was conducting my research, GPS was not commonly used. Recording of coordinates using GPS back then was considered at the very vanguard of research and I was among the first to use this technology in Saudi Arabia. However, just as my predecessors did with the astrolabe, I used GPS in consultation with other traditional tools and data. Thus, the technological aspect of my research was combined with more traditional disciplines, such as cartography (the science of drawing and reading maps), and I spent many years tracking down and acquiring old maps of the Arabian Peninsula. I trained myself to read and utilize them, and became adept at identifying the characteristics and criteria of a good map. With old maps, I was able to identify and retrieve much of what has been lost of historical places around Saudi Arabia. I could extract information about abandoned and deserted ruins and sites, and even discover places which are no longer extant. For example, through my study of historic maps, I was able to pinpoint exactly the old boundary of the Holy City of the Prophet (ﷺ).

I see fascinating parallels between my work using GPS and the functions and use of the astrolabe. In many ways, the astrolabe can be seen as an early form of GPS. Dr. Harold Williams, an American astrophysicist, stated that the astrolabe is "the most important astronomical calculating device before the invention of digital computers, and the most important observational astronomical device before the invention of the telescope" (Al Hassani. 2012, 280). Like the computer, the astrolabe has many functions and uses. In addition to establishing time and place, the astrolabe can also be used in geographical surveying which includes measuring the height of mountains and the depth of wells, as well as measuring buildings and monuments. Indeed, the 10th-century astronomer Abdulrahman Al-Sufi was known to have numbered 1,000 uses for the astrolabe (Al Hassani, 2012. 280).

Remarkably, this device not only determined the orientation of the mosque towards the qibla, but was used in the design and construction of buildings. As an architect and city planner, I hold a special appreciation for the versatility and historical importance of such an instrument. Equally, as a historian and geographer, and someone who has devoted his life to tracing the ancient migratory roots across the Arabian Peninsula, I consider the astrolabe immensely important both in relation to the history of Islam in particular and the history of the world in general.

Time and mosque

Muslims had a special penchant for making astronomical instruments, into which they poured their amazing talents, making works of art which distinctively combined beauty and function as seen in this astrolabe. These devices are scientific instruments of the highest order, as well as masterpieces of art and design.

The astrolabe was not the only instrument used by Muslims to determine time and place. Many historical mosques contain sundials in their courtyards (see Figure 1.4), or celestial globes (Figure 1.5) and quadrants in their storehouses. These instruments vary in degrees of precision and beauty. From mosque *waqfiyyas* (deeds), I learned that mosques often employed the services of timekeepers, or *miqatis*, who used these scientific devices to set the times for prayer and prompt the muezzin to call for prayer at the appointed time. As a prerequisite to their appointment as a timekeeper, they were expected to know "how to determine the sun's degrees during the day and the time of the rising of the stars at night" (the *waqfiyya* of the Ghuriyya complex 882, 182–3), and so would be knowledgeable about the use and application of various astronomical devices, including the planispheric astrolabe.

What I find particularly remarkable about the astrolabe is that the religious requirement to calculate accurate prayer times and determine the qibla drove the development of sophisticated scientific instruments in the Muslim civilization. These instruments, and the learning that went with them, had a massive impact on world history. It is well documented that Muslim Spain passed on the invention of the astrolabe to Christian Europe sometime in the 11th century, and this transfer of knowledge ultimately led to modern-day astronomy. Thus, satellite applications such as GPS and GIS technology were made possible by the accuracy and flexibility of the astrolabe, otherwise known as the "mathematical jewel." Arab scientists helped pave the way for the modern world as we know it.

1.4 **Sundial of the Great Mosque of Qayrawan, Tunisia**
A sundial located in the courtyard of the Great Mosque of Qayrawan, Tunisia, which was built in 670, making it one of the earliest mosques ever built.

Final words

Today, establishing the correct time and geographical location is something we generally take for granted. For those who have traveled to the remote and uninhabited places of the earth, as I have in the vast deserts of Arabia, the need to track time and place is of vital importance. I have found that, despite the advanced and widespread nature of satellite technology, my journeying would have gone awry without God's mercy and the help of local and expert guides who are able to navigate by reading the land and sky. I find it heartening that much of their traditional knowledge in navigation remains unchanged from that used by our Prophet (ﷺ) and his companion on that fateful journey. When most visitors come to the Hijaz, their destinations are Makkah and Medina, and whether they travel between these two cities by plane or by land, they do not get a sense of the Hijra. The actual Hijra route is off the highway, off the beaten track – it is truly the road less taken.

1.5 **Celestial Globe**
This celestial globe is decorated with images of constellations and planets as if earth were at the center of the globe, with the viewer observing from outside the sphere of the fixed stars.

Iran, 17th century
Copper alloy inlaid with silver
Height: 20 cm, Diameter: 15 cm
Museum of Islamic Art, Cairo 15226

1.6 **Compass**
The magnetic compass, engraved with the abjad system (letters replace numbers), was primarily used to find the qibla (direction of Makkah).

Iran, 19th century
Copper alloy, engraved and inlaid with silver, magnetic iron needle under glass
Depth: 1.7 cm, Diameter: 7.5 cm
Museum of Islamic Art, Cairo 15352

1.7 **Calendar Scroll**

Almanacs of this type are very rare and provide tables of times of prayer for each month of the solar year, as well as other times of religious importance.

Egypt, c. 1805
Ink and gold on paper
Length: 124 cm, Width: 11 cm
Museum of Islamic Art, Cairo 18188

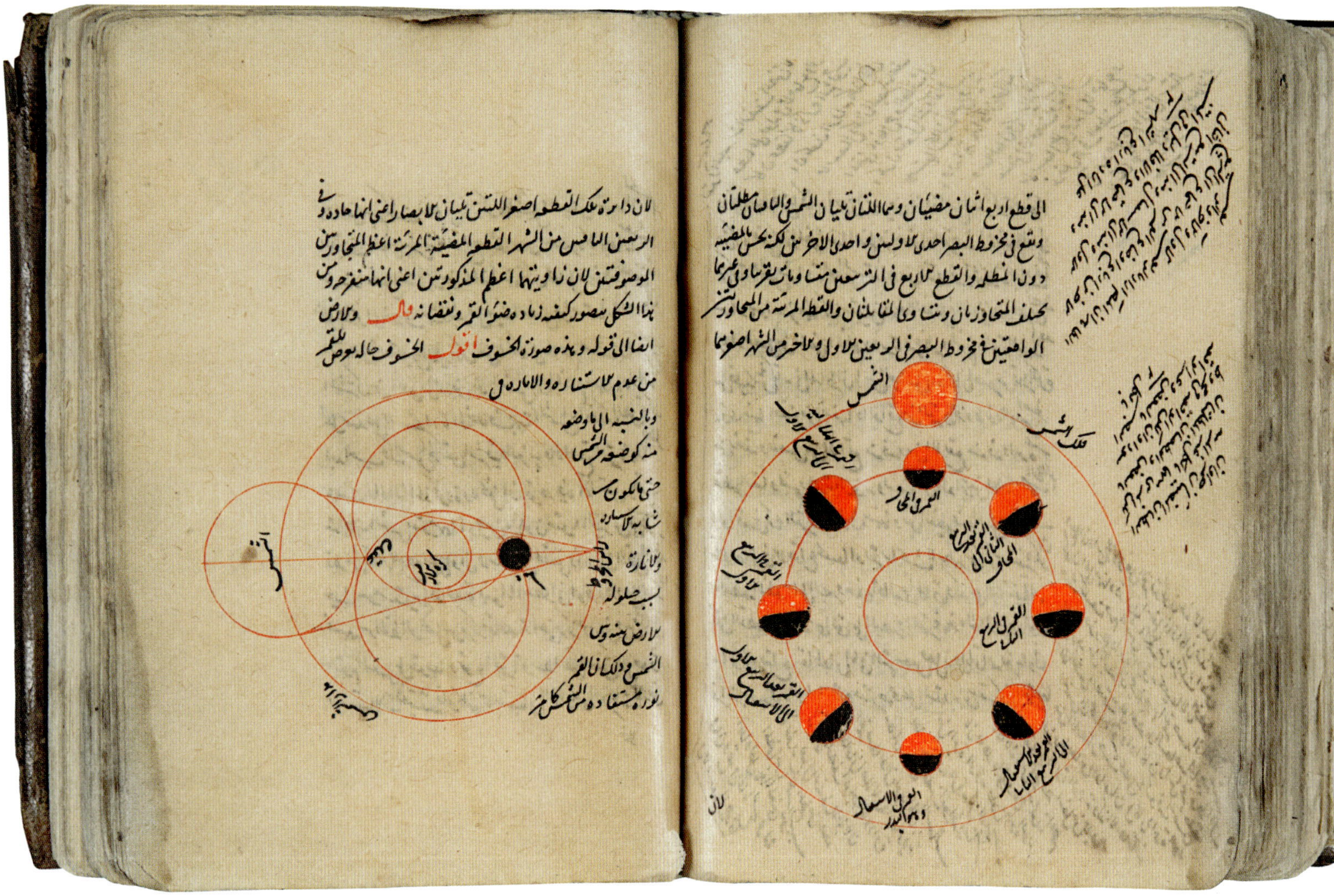

1.8 **Book on Astronomy**

This is a commentary by a well-known Persian astronomer named al-Nishapuri (14th century) on the *al-Tadhkirah fi 'Ilm al-Hay'a*, the seminal work on astronomy by the famous 13th-century astronomer Nasir al-Din al-Tusi.

Nishapur, Iran, 1490
Ink on paper
Height: 14.3 cm, Width: 9.7 cm
Ithra Museum 2020.0068

1.9 **Astrolabe**

In addition to its use in navigating on land and sea, this device was indispensable for mosques as it was used both to establish the exact direction of the qibla (Makkah) and to determine the times of prayer.

Egypt, 18th century
Copper alloy
Diameter: 15 cm
Museum of Islamic Art, Cairo. 4295

2 Masjid Al Nabawi: The Prophetic Prototype

Sami Angawi

I am blessed to have been raised in Islam's holiest site. I was born in Makkah Al-Mukaramah and my family have all had the privilege of being involved with the Hajj pilgrimage in various capacities. My father and grandfather come from a long line of *mutawwif* (guides for pilgrims).
As such, the memory of these holy places is a part of me, almost part of my genes. In the same way I inherited my physical features, it is my belief that I also hold an "inherited memory" of these holy places. Throughout my life's work researching the Hajj, Makkah and Medina, my mind is often brought back to some of my earliest memories from when I was a child. While I am immensely grateful for my upbringing, I realized very early on in my life that with these immense privileges comes great responsibility. As such, I have always felt it was my duty to study the Holy Sites of Makkah and Medina and ensure that their meaning and their significance continue to be researched for the benefit of the whole world.

← Detail of 2.2

2.1 **The Ka'ba in the Masjid al-Haram (the Holy Sanctuary) of Makkah**
Dating from the late 1800s, this black-and-white postcard shows the Ka'ba within the Masjid al-Haram (the Holy Sanctuary of Makkah) and its surroundings, which had, until then, changed very little for over half a millennium. Every mosque in the world is orientated towards the Ka'ba, and Muslims pray towards it.

Therefore, throughout the period of my studying architecture abroad during the 1970s, the cities of Makkah and Medina never once left my mind; in fact, the more I learned, the more I felt that the link and connection with these holy places grow and become stronger. Moreover, following the completion of my master's degree in the United States, and a period of working with some great architects of my generation – including Frei Otto from Germany, Hassan Fathi of Egypt and others – I became certain that I wanted to focus and devote my life to studying the Hajj in the context of the two Holy Cities of Makkah and Medina.

Researching the Hajj

For those unfamiliar with the Hajj, it is the pilgrimage to the Holy City of Makkah in Saudi Arabia, which every adult Muslim must make at least once in his or her lifetime. The pilgrimage rites which begin every year on the seventh day of Dhu al-Ḥijjah (the last month of the Islamic year) and ends on the twelfth day, comprises the fifth pillar of Islam after the *shahada* (declaration of faith), the five daily prayers, the payment of the charitable tax and fasting for the month of Ramadan. The Hajj rites, which were established by the Prophet Mohammed (ﷺ), started from Prophet Ibrahim's call on people to perform it. Then, during the time of Prophet Ismail, there came into being the profession of *mutawwif* to serve the pilgrims. To this day, we see large crowds of people from all over the world descend upon the two Holy Cities during the Hajj season.

Despite the important status of the two Holy Cities, and the Hajj being the largest gathering of people anywhere on the planet, it has always remained a seriously understudied subject both by Western scholars and those from within the tradition. History aside, I realized early on that very little knowledge or data existed in our modern times about Hajj as performed by millions of pilgrims who come to Makkah every year. Information was lacking for a full picture of the Hajj and to solve its problems, such as movement, the environment, the stones for the throwing ritual, the planning and other important inputs that should be taken into consideration alongside the social and economic profile of those coming, or the management the crowds during the Hajj. It was for those reasons that I founded the Hajj Research Center in 1975 at the King Abdulaziz University in Jeddah. Its mission was to study the Hajj in all its components, issues, system and aspects including, but not limited

2.2 **Kiswa Textile**
This textile is decorated with zigzag patterns and calligraphic inscriptions, including the declaration of faith: "There is no God but Allah" and the names "Allah" and "Mohammed" (ﷺ). It was hung on the interior walls of either the Ka'ba in Makkah or the Prophet's tomb in Medina.

Turkey, 19th century
Silk, embroidered with gold
Length: 200 cm, Width: 88 cm
2019.0032 Ithra Museum

to, sociological, historical, cultural, environmental issues and planning. A decision was issued by the cabinet in 1981 detailing the goals of the Center, which are:

1. Developing a data bank for pilgrimage to serve as a comprehensive scientific reference for all statistics and facts, and building a simulation model with figures for the various rituals of Hajj, thus helping immensely in planning.

2. Working on developing a historical record, complete with studies, documents, pictures, films, maps and historical manuscripts for Hajj and the two Holy Cities to be an established scientific and historical reference.

3. Maintaining the natural environment as created by God in the sacred places, and preserving the Islamic nature of the two Holy Cities of Makkah and Medina.

An important research aim for the Center was to address the Hajj through an integrated system that brought together various disciplines and specialisms. With support from the university and collaboration with other universities, we were able to bring specialists to the Center from around the world to consult and work with us on generating a massive amount of data and research on almost every aspect of the Hajj. The newfound field subsequently became known as "Hajjology."

The beating heart of the faith

Although I hold a special bond to Makkah, where I have been blessed enough to live and breathe this most holy of sites for Muslims, I also have an equally deep love for the Prophet's Mosque in Medina. It has a beauty and a significance which complement the site in Makkah and I believe that together these two blessed sites represent the beating heart of Islam.

This heart analogy can be taken further. The Prophet (ﷺ) himself described the *ummah*, the Islamic community, as one body with different parts. The Hajj can be seen as the lungs. The lungs bring air into the body so that the oxygen can clean and renew the blood cells. One can visualize the pilgrims walking around the Ka'ba during the Hajj. The arrival and movement of people from all over the world to Makkah reminds one of the circulation of the blood around the heart. They are like the blood cells, being renewed as they go around the heart. They are purified and renewed and in turn the whole body (Islamic world) is being renewed and regenerated. Pumped to the world purified. Cells are reborn.

Medina is an integral part of this beating heart. Pilgrims travel to Medina to visit the Prophet's Mosque and there is a deep love and emotion that pervades this Holy Site. While Makkah counts for far more in terms of remission of sins and performance of religious duty, I feel that Medina is characterized by a profound love and affection for Prophet Mohammed (ﷺ). Therefore, when pilgrims come to Medina, they know that they are entering the place where the Prophet (ﷺ) lived and where he built his house and mosque and there is a real feeling here that we are connecting with his life and work.

Thus, Medina's significance comes from its status as the first Islamic state during its rule by the Prophet (ﷺ). It was from this city that Islam first flourished and spread around the world a civilization that unites without discrimination or fanaticism, bringing a message of peace and mercy to the world. The city holds the first mosque in the world (the Quba Mosque), and the Masjid al-Qiblatayn (the Mosque of the Two Qiblas), wherein the direction of prayer (qibla) was switched from Jerusalem to Makkah. Most importantly however, the city holds the mosque where Prophet Mohammed (ﷺ) is buried and where his house stood (the Mosque of the Prophet). As such, the millions of pilgrims that travel to Medina every year do so to complete their Hajj although it is not a main part of the Hajj rites. Their visit is motivated by the love and affection they have for their Prophet (ﷺ) and they go to experience his presence and memory and for the blessing (*barakah*). In many ways, the pilgrim's journey from Makkah to Medina can be seen to mirror the Hijra (see Abdullah Alkadi's research in Chapter 1) and it is undertaken purely out of love for the Prophet, to see and experience the places where he lived and spent the last days of his life, and from where knowledge, science and the Islamic civilization blossomed.

The heart of the community

The Prophet's Mosque, or Masjid Al Nabawi, was built in 622 (the first year of the Hijri calendar) by Prophet Mohammed (ﷺ) and his companions. Since then it has been modified, rebuilt and expanded upon on a regular basis. Throughout the history of Islam, various dynasties and rulers have taken it upon themselves to extend, modernize and embellish the mosque and its surroundings. Each successive building scheme was mostly due to the ever-increasing numbers of worshippers to the mosque during the Hajj season. During the reign of the Rightly Guided Caliphs (*Rashidun*), the mosque was expanded twice, first by Omar ibn Al Khattab and then Uthman ibn Affan (may God be pleased with them). While the mosque today is very different from how it was during those early years, there is still something of the original structure. For example, some main pillars are still in the same location as they were, such as the Pillar of Repentance (*ustuwan al-tawbah*) or the Pillar of Deputations (*ustuwan al-wufud*), which are related to the different events in the Prophet's life. There are of course other parts which partially date back to the original structure, particularly those elements built around the final resting place of Prophet Mohammed (ﷺ) and his companions Abu Bakr and Omar (may Allah be pleased with them).

However, the original Prophet's house and mosque (shown in Figure 2.5, as it was in 632) was essentially a large enclosed space with the most significant feature of the building being a large empty courtyard which covered around 75 percent of the available space. The enclosing walls were comprised of plastered mud bricks (adobe). Along the inner wall next to the qibla which was indicated with a black rock and was the precursor for the *mihrab* niche – was the *zulla*, or shaded place, a double row of palm trunks carrying a roof of palm leaves. The *zulla* was large enough to accommodate over 100 worshippers during prayer.

2.3 **The Prophet's Mosque in Medina**
The famous green dome surmounts the final resting place of Prophet Mohammed (ﷺ). Originally the location of his wife Aisha's (may Allah be pleased with her) house, it correlates to number 13 on the plan shown in figure 2.5.

This open and covered courtyard space as modeled on the Prophet's Mosque in the seventh century was replicated by later mosques, such as those seen in Damascus (Syria) and Sammara (Iraq) which were built by the Umayyad and Abbasid dynasties respectively (see Figures 2.6 and 2.7).

Opposite in the northwest corner was another covered area, known as the *Suffah*, which was half as deep and less than half as long. It was built specially to shelter the most poor and destitute among the companions, who were named *Al-Suffah* after it. The courtyard held no other structures

and the three gates, from the west, north and east, gave it access to the courtyard. They were little more than openings in the wall.

The east side of the original Prophet's Mosque included the nine dwellings for the Prophet's wives, which were added to organically as his family grew. The mosque was adjacent to the dwellings and had different layers or sections. Within these layers was a public area (open to all), which included the main courtyard. Next came the semiprivate area, which comprised the area around the columns (*ustuwans*) of *Wufud*, *Haras* and *Sarir* (see Figure 2.5) immediately adjacent to the Prophet's dwellings, and then the private areas where the Prophet would be with his immediate family, including his daughter Fatimah and son-in-law Ali (may Allah be pleased with them). Finally, there is the area designated as "very private," which housed the Prophet and his wives.

Immediately around the mosque were the houses belonging to the Prophet's closest companions, including Abu Bakr, Uthman and Omar (may Allah be pleased with them). These dwellings and the areas surrounding them are considered an extension to the mosque, and were known to function as places to host and accommodate guests and visitors to the mosque. Thus, the Prophet's Mosque was a distinct entity and part of its surroundings at the same time. It was the nucleus around which the urban fabric of the city was formed, and its function should be understood in that context. It was the building's inclusivity that is so distinctive and characteristic of the early mosques in Islam. For example, we see something of this in the great mosque universities of Qarawiyyin in Fez (Morocco) or the Umayyad Mosque in Aleppo (Syria). Due to their close proximity with community housing, streets and markets, these mosques still echo something of the community spirit that was found in the Prophet's Mosque in Medina during the early period.

2.4 **The Tomb of Prophet Mohammed (ﷺ)**
The gold calligraphic grill and black curtains surround the area where Prophet Mohammed's (ﷺ) body lies. Millions of pilgrims visit this place every year, since it is a tradition to visit his mosque after the pilgrimage to Makkah.

Therefore, this building represented the Prophet's vision for how a mosque should be integrated with the wider community. The simplicity and austerity of its layout, as well as its flexibility in terms of its function, left an enormous mark on later mosques. What we learn from looking at the mosque constructed by Prophet Mohammed (ﷺ) is the importance of the mosque and its linking between faith and the daily life of citizens and the community. Its role included many religious, social, political, administrative and cultural functions. It became a model and template for all Muslim civilizations across the world.

2.5 The Original Prophet's Mosque in Medina

The rendering shows the original Prophet's Mosque after the qibla, or direction of prayer, was changed from Jerusalem to Makkah. Built by the Prophet Mohammed (ﷺ) and his companions in 622, this partially covered mosque comprised a simple mud-brick enclosure measuring approximately 50 × 50 meters. The layout rendered here is based on the latest research by Dr. Sami Angawi.

1 Smaller House of Uthman
2 Grand house of Uthman
3 House of Abu Ayyub al-Ansari
4 House of Al-Hasan
5 House of Omar ibn Al Khattab's family
6 Al-Tawbah (Pillar of Repentance)
7 Al-Sarir (Pillar of Al-Sarir)
8 Al-Wufud (Pillar of Deputations)
9 House of Abu Bakr
10 Gate of al-Rahmah
11 Courtyard of Masjid Al Nabawi
12 House of Hafsa
13 House of Aisha
14 House of Um Salama
15 House of Fatmah
16 House of Fatmah
17 Gate of Jibril
18 House of Zeinab Bint Jahsh
19 House of Jawayriah
20 Suffah
21 House of Ramla Bint Abi Sufian
22 House of Rabtah
23 House of Abu Bakr

The mosque and its many functions

The Prophet's Mosque was not only a place for individual and congregational worship, but was also a center for learning, the seat of the Prophet's government, a welfare and charity center and a place for medical treatment and nursing. Indeed, there was an area of the mosque that was reserved for people who required medical treatment. For example, when the wounded companions were brought back, they would be placed in a section inside the mosque. Some of the women would take care of them, not only treating their wounds, but also feeding them. For example, it was recorded that during the time of the Prophet, a female companion named Rufaydah used to nurse the sick people in the mosque of the Prophet. In her tent, pitched within the courtyard of the mosque, it was related that Rufaydah nursed one of Prophet's closest companions, Sa'd bin Mu'adh (a leading figure among the Ansar) following the Battle of the Trench (al-Khandaq). Subsequent generations never lost sight of this important function and we find in various mosque *waqfiyyas* (endowment deeds) that *tabib* or physicians were employed to examine and care for the sick and poor.

Of course, let us recall that some of the women did fight in the battles. The evidence suggests considerably less segregation of men and women than we might expect. Indeed, women played a very important role in both teaching and in caring for people. The Prophet's wives became students of the faith and then, in turn, teachers. The religion spread through their teaching and reached out to new converts through these women. The Prophet's Mosque also functioned as a school for the fledgling community in Medina. Indeed, the mosque facilitated every opportunity to acquire and share knowledge and the mosque's courtyard was often full of study circles over which the Prophet (ﷺ) often presided. Neither women nor children were overlooked in the process, and it was related that the Prophet (ﷺ) allocated time every week for teaching exclusively women (Hadith Sahih Muslim).

Culture and poetry were also present. For example, we have a famous account of a visiting group from Ethiopia performing a dance within the grounds of the mosque: the Prophet watched them and his wife Aisha (may Allah be pleased with her) lay her head on his shoulder. Moreover, Hassan Ibn Thabit, one of the most outstanding of all Arab poets, was known to have recited poetry inside the mosque and in the presence of the Prophet

2.6 **The Courtyard of the Great Mosque of Damascus, Syria**
Built by the Umayyad Caliph ʿAbd Al-Walid (r. 705–15), the courtyard and covered prayer hall of this hypostyle mosque are inspired by the layout of the original seventh-century Prophet's Mosque in Medina.

Mohammed (ﷺ) who once said to him: "O Hassan! Reply on behalf of Allah's Messenger. O Allah! Support him with the Holy Spirit" (Hadith al-Bukhari).

Another important function of the mosque was its role as the seat of the first Islamic government. In the mosque, the Prophet (ﷺ) used to hold daily meetings to decide on the many worldly affairs related to administering the state. It was also the place where he received foreign dignitaries.

The mosque every so often also served as a revenue and charity distribution center, and later even the place to house the treasury. Al-Bukhari narrates that the Prophet (ﷺ) brought in money from

2.7 **The Ruins of the Great Mosque of Samarra, Iraq**
Apart from the introduction of the spiral minaret, which is clearly based on the ziggurat of earlier Babylonian buildings, the Great Mosque of Samarra (built 848–51), which was then the world's largest mosque, was largely based on the layout and plan of the mosque built in Medina by Prophet Mohammed (ﷺ) and his companions.

Bahrain and said: spread it in the mosque. It was the biggest amount of money he had brought in. Then the Prophet led the prayer and did not look at the money. When he finished the prayer, he sat near the money and would not see anyone going by without giving them from it (Hadith al-Bukhari).

An example for life

What we see here through all the elements of the mosque complex is that the Prophet (ﷺ) took a holistic approach to life and faith. Islam is always seeking to build the community into a single body with a complete personality, addressing all the aspects of life. The Islamic faith, like the mosque, addresses the needs of the whole person. Therefore, while the worship in the Prophet's Mosque is the most important element, it was not the only one. The gathering, talking, interaction and sharing with each other were also key. It was a school, perhaps the first school which eventually developed into a university – indeed one Arabic term for mosque is *Jami'*, which shares a root with the Arabic word for university: *Jami'ah*. Thus, the mosque became a place for teaching, learning, sharing and reflection.

2.8 **The Interior of the Prophet's Mosque**
A man reads from the Holy Qur'an close to one of the oldest sections of the mosque known as the *Rawdah* (garden), which designates the sacred area between the Prophet's grave and his pulpit.

2.9 **Alem (Finial)**
Originally surmounting a minaret of the Holy Mosque in Makkah, this brass finial holds the crescent moon, which is a symbol of both the mosque and Islam.

Makkah, 17th century
Hammered copper
Height: 180 cm, Diameter: 32 cm
Ministry of Tourism of
Saudi Arabia 2476

I believe that the Prophet's Mosque can tell us a lot about finding balance and harmony in our lives. It represents the first and most important phase in the long evolution of the mosque. I like to differentiate here between evolution, which I regard as positive, natural and healthy, and change, which I think of as signifying some kind of break with the original. For example, when liquid water evaporates to steam, that is a form of evolution and it is natural. However, when water is contaminated with some other substance, then it is changed. And I regard that as something negative.

We see a good example of this positive kind of evolution with the Prophet's Mosque and its influence on later mosques. There have been modifications through the years, but these have been a natural evolution and development of the whole complex. Their essence and their essential purpose have been preserved through all the alterations and developments. We still see the integration with the wider community and this emphasis to make the faith about the whole life and the whole person. Therefore, the Prophet's Mosque is much more than a building. It is a lesson about the life and faith for all of us.

قدوة [illegible] عبد الرحيم [illegible] مشيخت [illegible]

شرفه:

[illegible] الصدارت

[illegible] عبد الرحيم

[illegible] مطلقا

[illegible]

وقرينه

عمره ١١٩٥

[illegible] ٢٨ م

[illegible]

3 The *Waqf* Firman: Everlasting Charity

Mona AlJalhami

> "O Beshir! Carry out good deeds. God forgives missteps."
> (Text from the *Waqf* of Beshir Agha, 1717)

There is a garden watered by a well in the northwest of Medina, approximately five kilometers from the Prophet's Mosque. This well and garden illustrate an important element of Islamic law and practice. For hundreds of years, locals and travelers have benefited from the well. But this was not always so.

Medina was previously called Yathrib. It was the city the Prophet (ﷺ) and the *Muhajireen* (emigrants) went to when they were evicted from Makkah. The people who warmly welcomed him in Yathrib were called *Ansar* (supporters) and many of them insisted on hosting the Prophet (ﷺ) during his stay. The Prophet (ﷺ) stayed at the house of Abu Ayyub al-Ansari for nearly seven months until the Prophet's Mosque and his house were built. Yathrib was known at the time for its shortage of fresh water. It was supplied by just one well. But this water was expensive, and it was a severe burden for the migrant companions who had left their houses and wealth behind in Makkah. It was claimed that the Messenger of Allah had promised a better well in Paradise for the one who would buy it for the believers in Yathrib (Hadith al-Bukhari). When Uthman ibn Affan (may Allah be pleased with him), the third wise caliph and close companion, heard about that, he asked the Prophet (ﷺ) if the word was true. Assured that it was indeed true, Uthman went to Rumah, the owner of the well, and bought it with a considerable amount of money. Uthman endowed it instantly for everyone in need, citizens or travelers (Hadith al-Bukhari). The area's gardens, farms and amenities were watered by Uthman's *waqf*: the well he had endowed.

This endowment was an early example of something which has become fundamental in Muslim culture. The use of endowments or donations, often by rich or royal pious believers, continued thereafter to establish some of the most iconic mosques and religious institutions as the faith spread.

← Detail of 3.1

The *waqf* (endowment)

The term *waqf* is now used to mean endowment in perpetuity. Its literal meaning in Arabic is "standstill" or *habs*, which means "inalienability or reservation" (Ibn Manzur, Lisan Al Arab). It is a voluntary and irrevocable dedication of one's wealth to God. The intrinsic characteristics of *waqf* that distinguish it from ordinary charity focus mainly on its permanence and the restrictions on gifting, selling or inheritance. *Waqf* institutions were establishments which were acknowledged, structured and protected by autonomous entities governed by Islamic jurisprudence, ensuring their permanent continuation.

In its simplest form, a *waqf* refers to an inalienable charitable endowment under Islamic law. It typically involves donating a building, a piece of land or an object for Muslim religious or charitable purposes. The donation cannot be revoked, even by the donor. And cannot be changed, even many years after the donor's death. *Waqf* records constitute veritable mines of historical data. Volumes of often copious detail were often appended to the original bequest which would describe actions and payments which arose from the endowment. For example, the *waqf* record for a mosque would include details of payments to custodians, cleaners, preachers and so forth, sometimes spanning several centuries.

*Waqf*s were enacted by both men and women. This short excerpt of a record details the expenditures of a wealthy woman's endowments for her village mosque under the Ayyubid dynasty, which ruled large areas of the Middle East in the 12th and 13th centuries. The text reads: "For the muezzin (prayer caller) each month is 20 dirhams and one pound of bread given daily and for the janitor 15 dirhams and one pound of bread given daily" (Al Shara'a. 2011, 152).

The use of the *waqf* extended and developed under the Mamluk period, as shown in the ledgers detailing the expenditures of the famous Sultan al-Ghuri complex located in Cairo and founded by Sultan Qansuh al-Ghuri. It contained a school, a library, a fountain and a khanqah, a form of meeting house. The document reads: "During the month of Ramadan a special expenditure totaling 11,000 dirhams should be made, the amount being distributed as follows: 1,200 dirhams should be given to the Imam; 4,800 dirhams are to be distributed among the teachers such that each receives 300 dirhams; 1,000 dirhams is to be given the prayer timer."

3.1 **Firman of Sultan Mustafa III**
This royal Ottoman decree of Sultan Mustafa III appoints Beshir Agha, the servant and keeper of the palace harem, as chief inspector of the *waqf* (endowments) of the Two Holy Mosques of Makkah and Medina and discusses their expenditures.

Istanbul, 1767
Gold on paper, with green, red and black ink
Length: 117 cm, Width: 50 cm
Ithra Museum 2019.0062

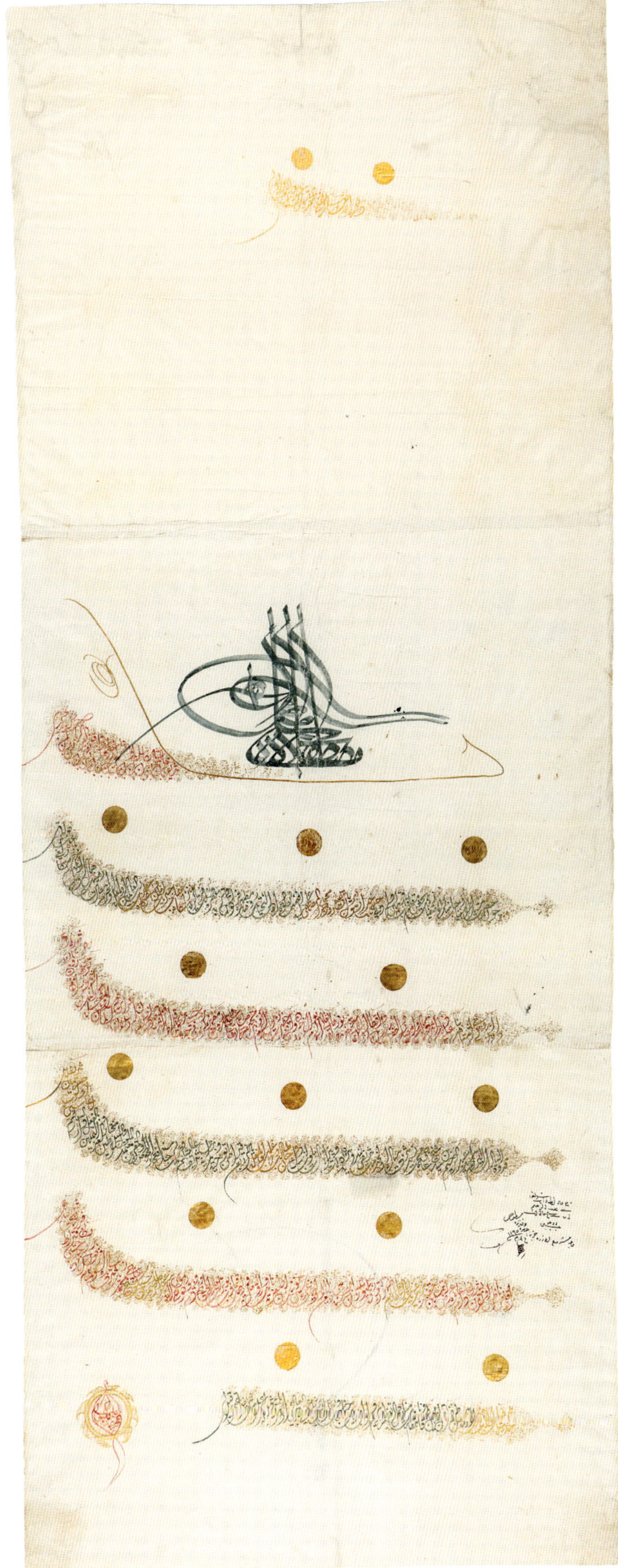

It added: "Three hundred dirhams to be given to the light keeper and his assistants; and 3,000 dirhams are to be expended on new clothing for the teacher, the overseer of orphans and the orphans. If after this, extra money is found, it should be spent for the needs of other orphans not resident in the complex" (Alhamzah. 2009, 28, 116).

As shown in the story of Uthman's *waqf*, a *waqf* need not refer to a mosque or even to a building. A *waqf* could bestow a well, a book, funding for doctors, a school or a field on successive generations. A *waqf* constitutes a special and noble calling enthusing the pursuit of good for all. "The believers in their mutual kindness, compassion and sympathy are just like one body. When one of the limbs suffers, the whole body responds to it with wakefulness and fever" (Sahih Al Bukhari). *Waqf* is every act of socioeconomic solidarity in the community realizing balance and inclusion, be it providing aid, development and elevation on all levels; benefiting both rich and poor.

3.2 **Seal of Beshir Agha**
On the bottom right of this manuscript is the seal of Beshir Agha admitting the volume as part of his charitable endowment. Inscriptions in the center state the date of endowment as 1745. The seal reads: "O Beshir! Carry out good deeds. God forgives missteps: Endowment for Allah."

Waqf records: markers of devotion

The early Islamic period saw the institution of the *waqf* take shape and flourish, particularly when it came to the establishment of mosques and bequeathing land. However, the need for more sophisticated and robust mechanisms quickly became apparent. Religious foundations such as schools and libraries continued to demand maintenance and upkeep. In addition, the area under Muslim rule continued to expand. This created a requirement to ensure and then regulate funding streams. This challenge was addressed through regulations on record-keeping under Islamic jurisprudence.

One of the first occurrences of seeking documentation in financial matters was under the rule of the wise caliph and close companion Omar ibn Al Khattab (may God be pleased with him) in 637. The event was chronicled by the ninth-century historian Al Tabari, who wrote: "In this year Umar assigned payments to Muslims and established the military registers. He determined the payments according to seniority according to Islam" (Al Tabari). This decision coincided with considerable wealth going to Medina as the territory under Muslim rule expanded. *Waqf* institutions constituted a form of public monetary institution and required clear procedures in monitoring and safeguarding wealth through documentation systems such as ledgers.

While there are thousands of *waqf* deeds preserved for posterity and which can be read and referenced today, many others are known only through references in other documents. For example, the Ottoman firman or imperial edict (Figure 3.1) by Sultan Mustafa III concerning the *waqf* of Makkah and Medina is a good example.

The edict dated 1181 AH (or 1767 CE) concerns Beshir Agha, who was a servant and keeper of the imperial Ottoman harem at that time. In the text, we read that the sultan places Beshir in charge of overseeing the endowments of the Two Holy Mosques covering the sanctuaries in Medina and Makkah. This was an enormous privilege, as well as a daunting responsibility.

The edict bears the distinctive tughra at the top, which was a form of the sultan's monogram in beautiful, stylized calligraphic fashion. The tughra was the stamp of legitimacy and authenticity in all Ottoman imperial decrees, and echoes the form of imperial Roman edicts in its use of the formula: "Mustafa Khan, son of Ahmed Khan, the always victorious." The green ink indicates the sultan's direction in matters of the Holy Sanctuaries and that explains why the tughra was green. This firman of Sultan Mustafa III is adorned with the elegant and majestic court script commonly used among Ottoman royalty. The text is artistically penned in a striking style in keeping with the grandeur of the Ottoman sovereign. There are other details which might not at first be apparent to the modern observer. For example, there is a large blank space at the top of the document. At the time of the firman's drafting, such a large space was indicative of the importance of the decree. An even larger blank space signified a more important firman.

As one of the curators of this exhibition, I consider myself blessed to have worked closely with this manuscript that carries so many memories of another age. One stands in awe contemplating these elegant lines of devotion displayed so beautifully. The significance of this firman is emphasized by the mention of the Two Holy Mosques and the spending of *waqf* funds. When considering this royal edict, one is spurred to dive deeper into the story and heritage behind this piece.

The sultan who ordered this edict, Mustafa III, was known for his efforts in reforming the internal affairs of the Ottoman Empire. He built hospitals and quarantine units across the country to contain epidemics widespread in his realm. He also built public libraries and established bridges to facilitate the transportation of goods and fresh water.

The six-line imperial edict, gilded and decorated with a variety of colors, promotes Beshir Agha, the servant and keeper of the palace harem, to take office as chief inspector of the *waqf*. He was responsible for the Two Holy Mosques of Makkah and Medina together with the Prophet's Sanctuary, where the Prophet Mohammed (ﷺ) was buried alongside two of his closest companions.

So who was Beshir Agha? And why was he addressed in a royal decree? In the book series Makers of the Muslim World, the author and academic Professor Jane Hathaway has written a volume on Beshir Agha. She specifically highlighted his long life and influential career in the Ottoman palace and court (Hathaway. 2012). Beshir came from a cohort of elite slaves who supervised the Ottoman palace harem; the word "Agha" was actually a title rather than a family name, despite the way it might appear to modern readers. This title of chief harem servant was created in the late 16th century and placed the chief agha third in power after the religious sheikh and the prime minister. This reflects the increasingly febrile situation in the court politics of the Sublime Porte, as the Ottoman imperial seat of government was known. Ambitious young sultans ascended to rule but died shortly afterwards, leaving only children as heirs to the throne. This left the empire in the hands of advisors such as the chief agha of the palace harem and the senior queen mother of the palace.

Because of the secluded lives which the sultans led in the late 16th and early 17th century, the chief servant of the palace harem was able to cultivate a public image, engage in social events and attend Friday sermons. They were also tasked with managing the finances generated by *waqf* revenue. The funds were spent on maintenance of the properties and on serving visitors. All these obligations gave the chief servant of the palace harem status and public influence as a religious figure.

The born survivor

There was a boy among a group of slave children who had already survived horrific conditions on a journey from Ethiopia to Cairo. Some of these children were destined for the royal court. Traveling alongside the Nile

3.3 **The Mosque of Beshir Agha in Istanbul**
Built in 1745, the exterior wall of the Beshir Agha Mosque contains a wall fountain (sabil), which provided passers-by with fresh water.

to the slave market, Beshir was purchased, along with some fellows, by none other than the wealthy Ottoman governor of Egypt. It was likely on his purchase in Cairo that this young boy was given the name of Beshir. In the governor's palace, he learned about Islam and began acquiring the principles of Ottoman court etiquette and service before being transported to Istanbul. Beshir Agha ascended in his 29 years of tenure from being a servant in the Ottoman palace harem to chief inspector of *waqf* at the Two Holy Mosques. He held the position of "Master of the Prophet's Sanctuary" as guardian of the Prophet's tomb, a tradition dating back to before the Mamluks. He traveled between Egypt, Medina, Makkah and Istanbul, passing the pilgrimage route, where he developed good ties with the people under his administration.

His job in the Ottoman palace, his close relationship with the mothers of the ruling sultans and his influence on education and upbringing affected the path of the empire. He witnessed some of the brutal court intrigues, as well as security problems. For example, in 1703, elements of the military mutinied in what became known as the "Edirne Event." In the aftermath of the revolt, Beshir Agha was part of the move to reform the civil administration, in particular ensuring that the sultan's most senior minister should not be in office longer than a year. He strove for peace in the Ottoman court, and facilitated and safeguarded the benefits and endowments of the Two Holy Mosques. In the book *Held in Trust*, Husam Abd Al Mu'ti tells us that Sultan Mustafa III created a small endowment that sent an annual sum of 36,900 paras to the Hijaz, of which 5,060 paras went to Makkah and 31,900 paras to Medina (Gazaleh. 2011, 92). This was one of many endowments managed under Beshir Agha's administration of the endowments of the Two Holy Mosques.

Beshir Agha escaped the fate of many who shared his office. He died of natural causes while still in office in Istanbul. We might conclude that his devotion towards his responsibilities somehow protected him from the political intrigues that caused many other senior figures to be either executed or exiled. He left as a legacy a number of pious initiatives in the service of the Almighty under endowment funding. These included a school in Medina and, as a tribute to his love of books, the famous library near the Asslam gate leading to the Prophet Mohammed's (ﷺ) sanctuary. Beshir Agha also founded public fountains and religious complexes, including one on the site of the Topkapi Palace in Istanbul, which included a book cabinet inside the building. His works included construction and maintenance of facilities across pilgrimage routes, as well as military deployments to protect the visitors to the Holy Sites.

There is a tremendous lesson in focusing on this *waqf* firman which highlights the Prophet's Mosque in Medina. This document takes us back to the life and work of the Prophet (ﷺ) himself. His whole life after Hijra was spent there where he practiced his supplications and prayers, met with the community, and discussed current events with his companions. The mosque he erected, the Prophet's Mosque, became the template for all mosques and served as a multipurpose community center. In the later stages, the mosque gave birth to classes, libraries, clinics and a soup kitchen, as well as leading to the development of architecture and art.

End of a tale

One of the many endowments established by Beshir lies in the Eyüp neighborhood of Istanbul at the burial site of Abu Ayyub al-Ansari, one of the Prophet's (ﷺ) companions and the person who hosted the Prophet (ﷺ) when he came to Medina. Beshir Agha endowed a small library with a school at the site to teach the Prophet's life and traditions.

3.4 **Water Fountain Basin**
Rulers and wealthy patrons provided their people with wells, cisterns and fountains, often attached to mosques. This distinctive Ottoman water fountain basin (sabil) is one such example.

Egypt, 18th century
Marble
Length: 94 cm, Width: 52 cm, Height: 58 cm
Museum of Islamic Art, Cairo 3993

Beshir Agha, who shared the same honor of serving the Prophet, was buried next to the companion of the Prophet.

The rise of Beshir Agha is truly an epic story in its own right. This is literally a tale of rags to riches, but also a story of faith and piety. He proved his character to be noble in the truest sense. When he was buried near Istanbul, the following inscription – found in the garden of Eyüp cemetery – was made in his honor (Akakus. 1973, 190; Demiriz. 1982, 38–9):

> He behaved as a slave to the summons to prayer.
> When he left the world, his excellency found another position.
> For when he realized that the happiness of the world was not everlasting,
> See the sincerity with which he set out on his final journey.
> A resting place was made for him near to Khalid Abu Ayyub al-Ansari.
> May God forgive his sins.
> May his place be in the Paradise of his companions, the men of learning.

3.5 **Water Fountain Basin**
Although its original setting is not known, this beautifully carved fountain basin would have been found in a public area such as the courtyard of a mosque or madrasa.

Egypt, 14th–15th century
Marble
Diameter: 47 cm, Height: 47 cm
Museum of Islamic Art, Cairo 3724

3.6 **Water Jar and Stand**
Pious Muslim leaders and wealthy individuals generously provided water dispensers, such as this one, in mosques and other public buildings, often as part of a *waqf* (endowment).

Egypt, 14th century
Marble
Diameter: 45.5 cm, Height: 79 cm (jar). Height: 40 cm, Depth: 55 cm, Width: 27 cm (stand)
Museum of Islamic Art, Cairo 3110 (stand) 123 (jar)

3.7 **Water Jar and Stand**
This *kilga* water jar and stand, dating from the Fatimid and Mamluk periods respectively, are carved from two blocks of marble. They provided water to the public for centuries.

Egypt, 14th century (stand),
11th century (jar)
Marble
Height: 48 cm, Depth: 75 cm, Width: 48 cm (stand)
Height: 79 cm, Depth: 45.5 cm (jar)
Museum of Islamic Art, Cairo
104 (stand) and 6921 (jar)

3.8 **Water Filters**
Originally found on the neck of large water jars, these filters were designed to keep water free from dirt and large insects.

Egypt, 14th century
Glazed ceramic
Diameters: 8 cm
Museum of Islamic Art, Cairo
13/19180, 22/19180, 4/19180

3.9 **Ewer and Basin of Amir Tabtaq**
This elegant ewer and basin set is inscribed with the name and insignia of the Mamluk Amir Tabtaq. He was the governor of Qus in Upper Egypt during the reign (1309–40) of the renowned Sultan al-Nasir Muhammad ibn Qalawun.

Egypt, 14th century
Brass, inlaid with silver, gold, copper and niello
Height: 40 cm,
Diameter: 15 cm (ewer)
Height: 18.2 cm,
Diameter: 15 cm (basin)
Museum of Islamic Art, Cairo
24084 (ewer) and 2/24085 (basin)

3.10 **Ewer**

The production of ewers originally flourished in Persia and was later transferred to Iraq and Egypt during the Ayyubid and Mamluk periods. They had different forms and functions. They were used to pour water for bathing and for the ablutions before prayer. As such, they were commonly found in mosques.

Egypt or Syria, 14th century
Brass
Height: 31 cm
Museum of Islamic Art, Cairo 24070

3.11 **Ewer and Basin**

The basin and ewer are engraved with the maker or owner's mark and the date AH 1248 (1832 CE). The ewer would be used to rinse the hands before and after meals, and the basin would collect the residue. The ewer often held scented rosewater.

Iran or Turkey, 1832
Tinned Copper
Height: 36 cm (ewer), Height: 9.4 cm, Diameter: 34 cm (basin)
Ithra Museum 2019.0051 (small cup), 2019.0055 (basin), 2019.0056 (ewer)

3.12 **Water Basin**
Probably made to accompany a ewer, this Mamluk-era basin is marked with prominent honorific titles signifying that it was made for a high-ranking noble.

Egypt, 15th century
Brass
Diameter: 40.6 cm
Museum of Islamic Art, Cairo 9315

3.13 **Stamp**

Inscribed with the words: "Allah is the greatest protector," this stamp may have been used by court administrators on official documents relating to the expenditure of mosque endowments (*waqfiyyas*).

Egypt, 12th century
Wood
Height: 7 cm, Length: 4.5 cm
Museum of Islamic Art, Cairo 14673

100 %

3.14 **Four Dinars**

This selection of gold dinars all date from different Islamic periods and are either inscribed with the name of the ruler and/or the profession of faith (*shahada*). The high value of these gold coins meant that they were not used in daily transactions but were more likely used for large charitable endowments to fund institutions such as mosques.

Egypt, Umayyad period, eighth century (a); Egypt, Abbasid period, late ninth century (b); Egypt, Ayyubid period, 12th century (c); Egypt, Mamluk period, 14th century (d)
Gold
Diameters: 1.5 cm
Museum of Islamic Art, Cairo
17575\13, 18496, 10803\6, 18470/3

a b
c d 100 %

3.15 **Pillar from the Holy Mosque in Makkah**
This octagonal pillar bears the name of the Mamluk sultan who endowed and oversaw the restoration and expansion of the Holy Mosque in Makkah.

Makkah, 1310
Carved marble
Height: 136 cm, Width: 50 cm
Ministry of Tourism of Saudi Arabia 2499

3.16 **Foundation Panel**
Probably attached to a mosque or a madrasa, this panel records the restoration of a sabil (water fountain) by someone named Ibrahim "seeking to do a good deed." It demonstrates the long Islamic tradition of maintaining water fountains for the benefit of the public.

Egypt, 17th century
Ceramic, underglaze-painted
Length: 20 cm, Width: 28 cm
Museum of Islamic Art, Cairo 4578

3.17 **Foundation Stone**

Known for his charitable endowments to various mosque complexes, the name of the Mamluk Sultan Qansuh al-Ghuri is inscribed on this foundation stone, which records the construction of a gate in the Egyptian city of Tanta.

Tanta, Egypt, 1505-6
Carved marble
Height: 84 cm, Width: 50 cm
Museum of Islamic Art, Cairo 13734

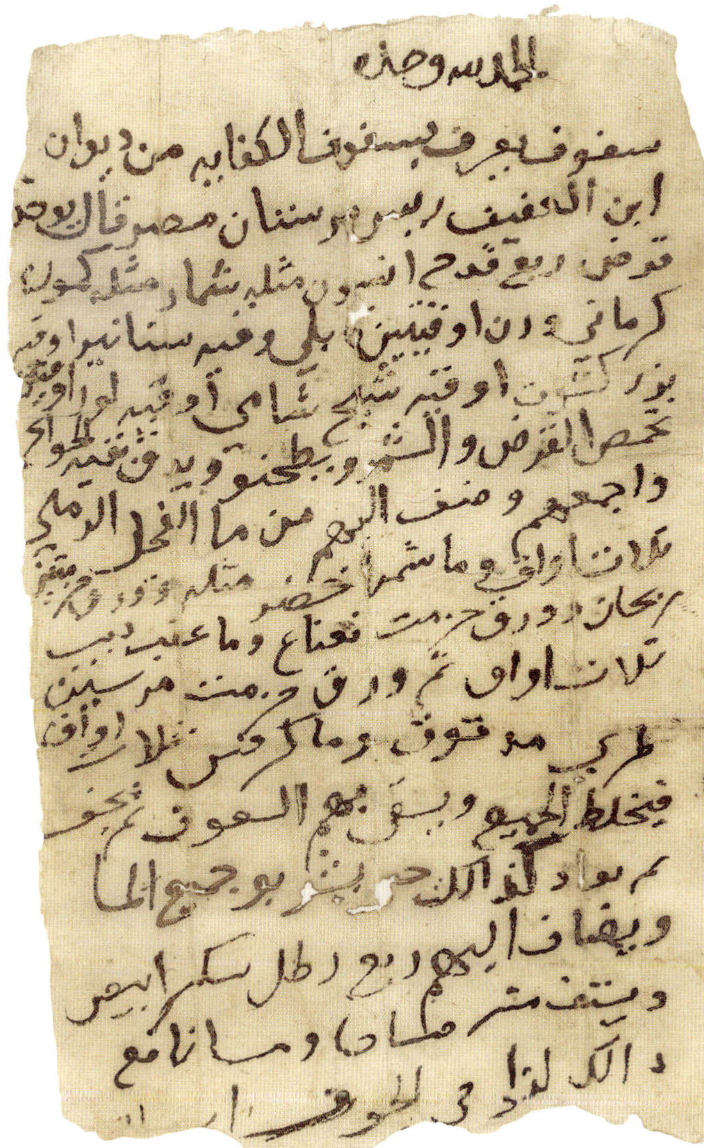

3.18 a

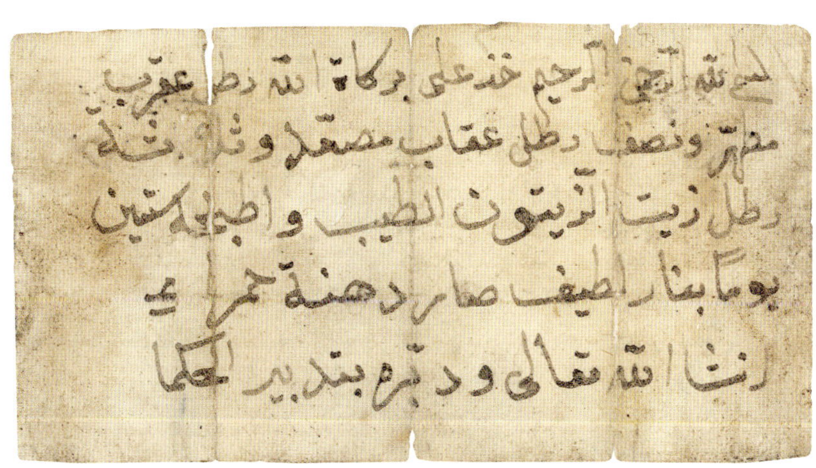

3.18 b

3.18 **Medical Prescriptions**
Mosque endowments often record the employment of doctors to prescribe medicine to orphans and the destitute. Hospitals adjacent to mosque complexes were usually funded by these same endowments. The prescription (above) describes a treatment for celiac disease and was written by Shams Al-Din ibn Al-'Afif, who was the head of the hospital of Sultan Qalawun.

Fustat, Egypt, 15th century (a);
Egypt, late ninth–12th century (b)
Paper and black ink
Width: 10 cm, Height: 16 cm;
Length: 11 cm, Width: 8 cm
Museum of Islamic Art, Cairo
9971, 25269

3.19 **Book on Medicine**

First part of the illustrated book *Kitab Al-Hasha'ish* (Book of Herbs) by Abu Ja'far al-Ghafiqi (d. 1165), a famous pharmacist and botanist from Andalusia.

His book was a resource for many doctors aiding the well-being of the community and would have been copied and placed into mosque libraries.

Istanbul, 1582
Paper with ink
Width: 27 cm, Height: 14.5 cm
Museum of Islamic Art, Cairo 3907

3.20

3.21 a

3.21 b

3.20 **Ladle**
This simple measuring ladle was most likely used together with other instruments to serve medicine in public hospitals or mosque clinics set up to serve the poor and needy.

Egypt, 19th–early 20th century
Silver
Length: 22.7 cm, Diameter: 6.1 cm
Ithra Museum 2019.0054

3.21 **Crystal Container and Stick**
This Fatimid-era rock crystal container was used to hold either medical or cosmetic liquids, such as kohl (stibnite) to cure ocular disease. The stick was used for application.

Egypt, 11th century (container); 19th century (stick)
Rock crystal; bone
Height: 7 cm (rock crystal),
Length: 5 cm (bone)
Museum of Islamic Art, Cairo
15446, 3/2259

3.22 **Bowl**
As part of their charitable role, mosques often serve food and operate soup kitchens. Although very ornate and probably belonging to a Fatimid noble, this bowl helps us to understand the shape and size of bowls in which food was traditionally served.

Egypt, 11th century
Diameter: 30 cm
Glazed ceramic
Museum of Islamic Art, Cairo 14850

3.23 **Bowl**

This Chinese-made bowl and cover contain short chapters from the Holy Qur'an, including Surat al-Fatiha, al-Ikhlas, al-Falaq and al-Nas, which are interspersed with stars and crescent-moon motifs.

China, 19th century
Glazed ceramic
Diameter: 15 cm, Height: 12 cm
Museum of Islamic Art, Cairo 6296

3.24 Foundation Stone of the Prophet's Mosque *Mihrab*

The inscription on this white marble foundation stone explains that the Mamluk Sultan Qaytbay gifted a prayer niche (*mihrab*) to the Prophet's Mosque in Medina. The gift of the *mihrab* was one part of the late 15th-century restoration of the mosque.

Medina, 1484
Carved marble
The Ministry of Tourism of Saudi Arabia 1-03-1-000802

صاحب الخيرات
محمد اغا

4 The Mosque Tile: Visualizing the Two Holy Sanctuaries

Raeda Ashour

I have always been captivated by all aspects of Islamic art, from architecture to geometry, calligraphy and miniature painting. However, perhaps because of my background, I have always held a special fascination for historic depictions of the Two Holy Mosques of Makkah and Medina. These diverse images are mostly found in manuscripts dealing with the pilgrimage or with the history of the Holy Cities and in Hajj certificates, prayer books and ceramic tile manuscripts. Looking at these "*Haramayn* images" has always given me a deep sense of belonging and identity. Ultimately, this propelled me to create a new art inspired by these images. It quickly became a passion of mine and I have created numerous works depicting the Holy Mosques of Makkah and Medina using techniques like photo-printing, manual embossing and traditional painted illumination. One of my aims is to maintain and preserve this important artistic tradition by reproducing these old images in contemporary colors and styles that can be appreciated by the modern viewer. Aware that these historic depictions that inspire my work represent spiritual subjects very close to the hearts of all Muslims, and were painted with great devotion by the master painters and craftsmen of their time, I try to convey the same spirit in my own work.

Before you (opposite) is one of those depictions; it comprises a 17th-century (1663) underglaze painted tile that depicts the Holy Sanctuary of Makkah, or Masjid al-Haram in Arabic. The tile was originally embedded in the wall of the Turkish mosque built sometime in the early 17th century. At the top runs the declaration of faith, the *shahada*: "There is no God but Allah and Mohammed is His Messenger," while at the bottom, one can find name of its maker, Aḥmad, as well as its tile's owner's name on the left: Muhammad Agha. The structures around the Ka'ba are all carefully labeled, including clusters of jugs used to collect water from the Holy *Zamzam* well.

← Detail of 4.1

The *Haramayn* illustrations: a historical context

In addition to creating depictions of the *Haramayn*, I also began to compile an image catalogue taken from different historic sources and collections.

I continue to be surprised by the variety of styles and colors of each new depiction I come across. Some of the earliest examples of these tiles were produced in the reigns of Ottoman sultans during the second half of the 16th century, who oversaw one of the most creative periods in the history of Islamic art. This was the time of the greatest and most recognized Ottoman architects and artists of the premodern Ottoman Islamic period. The art of this era reflected the multicultural nature of Ottoman society, which drew in influences from the various areas where the Turks had lived and several neighboring cultures. The nomadic, central Asian origins of the Ottomans themselves were key: "Artistic styles were absorbed through conquest, through direct invitations of artists, or through the migration of peoples" (Bierman et al. 1).

The Ottoman sultans, especially Suleiman the Magnificent, encouraged and commissioned artists. In 1575, he ordered the creation of works by approximately 898 artists. The sultan's palace was a center for artistic activity. From the 16th century onwards, illustrations depicting the Holy Sanctuaries in Makkah and Medina became more widespread in Ottoman art and appear in different forms, on Hajj certificates, prayer manuscripts and tiles. The tiles were publicly displayed in mosques and could therefore be seen by the masses. According to Maury's research, this tile is among 60 surviving examples, including 19 tiles still preserved in monuments in Turkey (Maury, 2013, 143). The two Turkish cities of Iznik and Kutahya, famous centers of the ceramic industry, competed in their production.

The illustrations that appear on the tiles are taken from Hajj certificates and other illustrated manuscripts that are related to Hajj, in particular *Futuḥ al-Ḥaramayn* by Muḥyi al-Din Lari (d. 1526) and the *Dala'il al-Khayrat* by Al-Jazuli (d. 1465). The first, *Futuḥ al-Ḥaramayn*, or *Revelations of the Two Sanctuaries*, was composed in Persian, and comprises a guidebook describing the Holy Cities of Makkah and Medina. The manuscript presented Muslim pilgrims with detailed instructions on the rituals of Hajj, both compulsory and voluntary, in precise order. It also contained a detailed list of religious sites they could visit in the region. The many copies of the manuscript, some of which were actually produced in Makkah itself,

4.1 **Tile Depicting the Holy Mosque of Makkah**
Originally placed into a wall of a mosque, this tile depicts the Holy Sanctuary of Makkah with the Ka'ba at its center. Probably made to commemorate a pilgrimage to Makkah, this tile bears the name of its owner, Muhammad Agha, who may have commissioned the mosque to which this tile originally belonged.

Egypt or Turkey, 1663
Fritware, painted under glaze
Width: 35 cm, Height: 38 cm
Museum of Islamic Art, Cairo 3251

اشهد ان لا اله الا الله اشهد ان محمد الرسول الله
صاحب الخيرات
محمد اغا
الواقع في سنة ١٠٧٤
عمل
احمد

included marvelous illustrations of the Two Holy Mosques and, in some cases, the complete order of the Hajj rituals.

The second example is the *Dala'il al-Khayrat*, or *Guidelines to the Blessings and the Shining of Lights, giving the saying of the blessed prayer over the chosen Prophet*, which consisted of prayers in honor of the Prophet Mohammed (ﷺ), as well as descriptions of sites in Makkah and Medina. Similarly, the *Dala'il Khayrat* was used as a Hajj guide by pilgrims from all over the Islamic world and has widespread popularity even to this day. The folio shown in Figure 4.2 is from an 18th-century version of the text and was produced in India. It depicts the sanctuary in Medina and would have originally been placed next to an adjoining illustration of Makkah. Like the image used in the tile, it gives a two-dimensional view and includes a representation of the Prophet's Mosque highlighting five minarets. Other details within the illustration include the Prophet Mohammed's (ﷺ) *minbar* (pulpit), *mihrab* (prayer niche), the tomb of Fatimah (may God be pleased with her) and the *rawdah*, or garden, where we find the tombs of the Prophet Mohammed (ﷺ) in addition to those of the Caliphs Abu Bakr and Umar (may God be pleased with them). Depicted in the lower section is the orchard of the Prophet Mohammed (ﷺ) with palm trees, and a circle representing a well in the garden of Fatimah (may God be pleased with her).

4.2 **Page from the *Dala'il al-Khayrat***
Rendered in a two-dimensional view, this painting from a copy of the *Dala'il al-Khayrat* (Waymarks of Benefits) includes a representation of the Prophet's Mosque, including his *minbar* (pulpit), *mihrab* (prayer niche) and the Rawdah (lit. "garden") adjacent to the tombs of Prophet Mohammed (ﷺ) and his companions Abu Bakr and Umar (may Allah be pleased with them).

India, 18th century
Ink, opaque watercolor and gold on paper
Height: 17 cm, Width: 10 cm
Ithra Museum 2019.0001

In another 18th-century example of the *Dala'il Khayrat* illustration presented in Figure 4.3, we see a double-page depiction of the Prophet's Mosque in Medina, rather than the customary coupling with the Masjid al-Haram in Makkah. This highly abstract depiction, which shows the *minbar*, *mihrab* and the Prophet's spear (*harba*) in addition to five minarets, was produced in Harar in Ethiopia. According to inscriptions found inside the book, the names and titles of the owner indicate that this copy was made for a minor ruler or chieftain in the service of the Ethiopian emperor.

What is evident from these illustrations is that they took the local style of the place in which they were produced. For example, the illustration found in Figure 4.2 shows onion-shaped domes and patterns which are characteristic of the Indian Mughal style. The result was a wealth of unique *Ḥaramayn* depictions.

Such manuscripts prefigure the guidebooks known today as *manasik* which are important tools for assisting pilgrims in undertaking their Hajj. They provide them with descriptions of the prayers and rituals, as well as their

meanings and significance. Pilgrims study these before departure and keep the text with them during Hajj.

The Hajj certificate

Finally, these *Haramayn* depictions were displayed on Hajj certificates. These certificates were traditionally granted to pilgrims, attesting that they had completed the Hajj, and they normally contained illustrations of the major pilgrimage sites in Makkah and Medina. Although "the primary importance of the Hajj certificates lies in their documentary value," due to "their artistic content they also enrich the field of Islamic Art" (Ulrich. 2014, 1). For me, these certificates are particularly special and they have inspired me to preserve and recover this no longer extant tradition through my art. Their inspiration is directly linked to my performing Hajj, which is one of the strongest spiritual experiences in my life and naturally the life of every Muslim. As I became so passionate about the experience, I wanted to keep it vivid in my mind and in my daily life. Having a Hajj certificate is a way of keeping the experience alive. Historic examples of Hajj certificates

4.3 **Page from the *Dala'il al-Khayrat***
Originally made for an Ethiopian chieftain, this copy of the *Dala'il al-Khayrat* (Waymarks of Benefits) contains a highly abstract illustration of the Prophet's Mosque in Medina depicting the Prophet's tomb, *minbar* and spear, as well as minarets. The manuscript consists of prayers in honor of the Prophet (ﷺ), for each day of the week, and describes Holy Sites in Makkah and Medina.

Ethiopia, probably Harar, 1750–1800
Ink and opaque watercolor on paper
Height: 23 cm, Width: 16 cm
Ithra Museum 2019.0011

were beautifully illustrated and decorated by illuminated calligraphy of the Qur'an or Hadith of the Prophet Mohammed (ﷺ) related to Hajj. Some took the form of scrolls, with one example being over seven meters long, while others were drawn horizontally. Because Hajj is a great spiritual event in the life of a Muslim, some wealthy pilgrims hired artists to accompany them on their journey to draw and document the event, to keep the memory alive throughout their lives.

My research has found a variety of certificates from different periods and places across the Islamic world. For example, I have found certificates that can be attributed to Indonesian, Indian, Ottoman and Qajari artists in museums around the world, including the British Museum, the Agha Khan Museum in Toronto and the Turkish and Islamic Art museum in Istanbul.

Roles and functions

These images of the Holy Mosques, in particular those depicted on the tiles, played many important roles for premodern Muslim viewers. They made the images of Makkah and Medina accessible for the common viewer. The tiles stood as reminders of the Hajj, the pilgrimage to Makkah that all Muslims should perform once in a lifetime provided that they can afford it. As Inay and Oguz have suggested, these tiles also occupied an important place in Islamic art because they offered a journey in a symbolic form for those who cannot afford to travel (Inay and Oguz. 2013, 43). The tiles were also educational tools, offering clear information and depictions of the Holy Sanctuary, thereby helping pilgrims better prepare for their Hajj. And if they had been donated to the mosque by a pious person (perhaps after having performed Hajj), the tiles commemorated the memory of the donor and were to be placed beside the *mihrab* facing towards the qibla. The tiles sometimes contained inscriptions asking the viewer to "remember the owner through prayer" (Maury, 2013, 147). These tiles often included verses from the Holy Qur'an, sayings of the Prophet (ﷺ) or poetry, all related to Hajj.

Education, inspiration and well-being

It is my opinion that this tile tells us something significant about Islamic art, namely the importance of art education for the well-being of Muslim society. This Ka'ba tile is a beautiful piece of art that was once presented on the wall of a mosque. The existence of such sophisticated works of art, besides fine ornamentation and calligraphy, as part of the interior design of mosques turned these buildings into a kind of "art gallery" that was integrated into the structure of everyday Muslim life. As such, they became centers for aesthetic education. Muslims were privileged to have such a nourishing environment all around them.

In my study of art and its impact on people, I have come across a lot of research that demonstrates the ability of art to shape our perception, refine our senses and enhance our imagination. For example, David N. Perkins, professor of education at Harvard, argues that observing art increases the quality of thinking (Perkins, 1994). In *The Arts and Creation of Mind*, Elliot Eisner, professor of art and education at Stanford, discusses the effect of art on human consciousness. He observes that "The arts have distinctive contributions to make. I count among them the development of the thinking skills in the context of an art form, the expression of communication of distinctive forms of meaning, meaning that only artistically crafted forms can convey, and the ability to undergo forms of experience of a consummatory nature, experience that can be secured when one attends to the world with an aesthetic frame of reference and interacts with forms that makes such experience possible." (Eisner. 2005, xii). Eisner also mentions the role of art in refining the senses and enhancing the imagination (p. 4). The developmental psychologist Howard Gardner notes how art education can be "a vehicle for promoting self-expression, imagination, creativity and knowledge of one's affective life" (Gardner. 2008, 35). In *Inner Vision: An Exploration of Art and the Brain*, the neuroscientist Professor Semir Zeki explores neural activity in relation to visual/artistic elements. In an interview, Zeki says that what happens in the brain when we view art is more than good for our health and can have a big impact on a nation's happiness. He argues that viewing art can give as much pleasure as being in love (ArtFundUK, 2011).

More generally, there are studies that show the benefits of art to mental and physical well-being and that visual art can have a positive effect on people by reducing stress, "increasing self-reflection and self-awareness, altering behavior and thinking patterns, and also by normalizing heart rate, blood pressure, or even cortisol levels" (Bolwerk et al., 2014, 1).

4.4 **Painting of the Masjid al-Haram (Holy Sanctuary of Makkah) by Raeda Ashour**
This painting of the Masjid al-Haram, the Holy Sanctuary of Makkah, was inspired by the 17th-century tile presented in this chapter (Figure 4.1).

Saudi Arabia, 2018
Manual embossing on paper, watercolor, pastel and gold leaf
Height: 100 cm, Width: 70 cm
Private collection

Such research also applies to the mosque environment and the scholar Ad-Darsh concludes that since believers frequent these places of worship at least on a weekly basis, they represent the perfect place "to instill all those precious artistic and ornamental values" (Ad-Darsh. 2019, 108). Similarly, Norhayati Kassim, Nora'shikin Abdullah and Zafrullah B. Mohammad Taib have highlighted more generally that "the role of Islamic decoration is varied, it can be spiritual, educational, social and psychological" (Norhayati et al. 2014, 57).

Thus, Islamic art and architecture have provided a positive daily exposure to beauty, pleased the eye and improved and refined the senses. They have developed cognitive abilities, enhanced spirituality and provided peace and tranquility. If looking at beauty affects the brain and emotions, then a visit to a mosque or the attentive reading or browsing of an illuminated Qur'an could provide well-being benefits as effective as a visit to a museum or an art gallery, in addition to the spiritual aspects specific to the faith.

Final words

As an artist, I am deeply affected by the Islamic aesthetic environment, particularly in the context of the mosque. Reflecting on this Makkah tile, I am reminded of the authentic Hadith from the Prophet Mohammed (ﷺ): "Allah is beautiful and He loves beauty." This statement for me reflects the traditional Islamic attitude towards art. The Divine and the beautiful in Islam are intertwined. I have come to recognize that identifying the particulars of Muslim values may strengthen my bond to Islamic art. In different forms of Islamic art and in their variety of expressions, individual Muslim artists reflect their own backgrounds yet express shared content.

Prompted by this tile to reflect on the wonders of Islamic art, I am moreover reminded that Islamic art no longer receives the recognition and attention it deserves, even from within the cultures and tradition for which it was made. To overlook the genius and benefits of Islamic art is to neglect one of the most attractive and accessible features of Islamic culture. To borrow the words of the scholar Rabah Saoud: "One area where Muslim genius has been recognized worldwide is that of art. Muslim artists adapted their creativity to evoke their inner beliefs in a series of abstract forms, producing some amazing works of art" (Saoud. 2004, 1). Moreover, in his book *Journey to Makkah*, Murad Wilfried Hofmann, a German convert to Islam, writes that Islamic art played a significant role in his becoming a Muslim. Hofmann notes "the tangible effect which Islamic harmony, the Islamic way of life, and the Islamic treatment of spaces leave on both heart and mind" (Hofmann. 1998, 33). Likewise, in his book *Art of Islam*, the scholar Titus Burckhardt, another convert to Islam, writes: "It is not surprising, nor strange that the outward manifestation of a religion or a civilization like Islam – and art is by definition an exteriorization – should reflect in its own fashion what is most inward in that civilization" (Burckhardt. 2009, xiv).

To conclude, I believe the strength and majesty of Islamic art stems from its spiritual sources. My aim is to indulge the visual tastes of my audience and at the same time uphold their spiritual and human values. Like other Islamic artists I try to emphasize in my work the sense of pride I feel for both my heritage and identity.

4.5 **Tile Depicting the Holy Mosque of Makkah**
From the 16th century onwards, Ottoman tile makers excelled at producing topographical depictions of the Holy Sanctuary of Makkah. Such tiles were sometimes placed on qibla walls since they represented the Ka'ba: the direction of the qibla.

Egypt or Turkey, 17th century
Fritware, painted under glaze
Width: 35 cm, Height: 38 cm
Museum of Islamic Art, Cairo 860

جبل عرفات
جبل طور
باب صفا
باب سلام

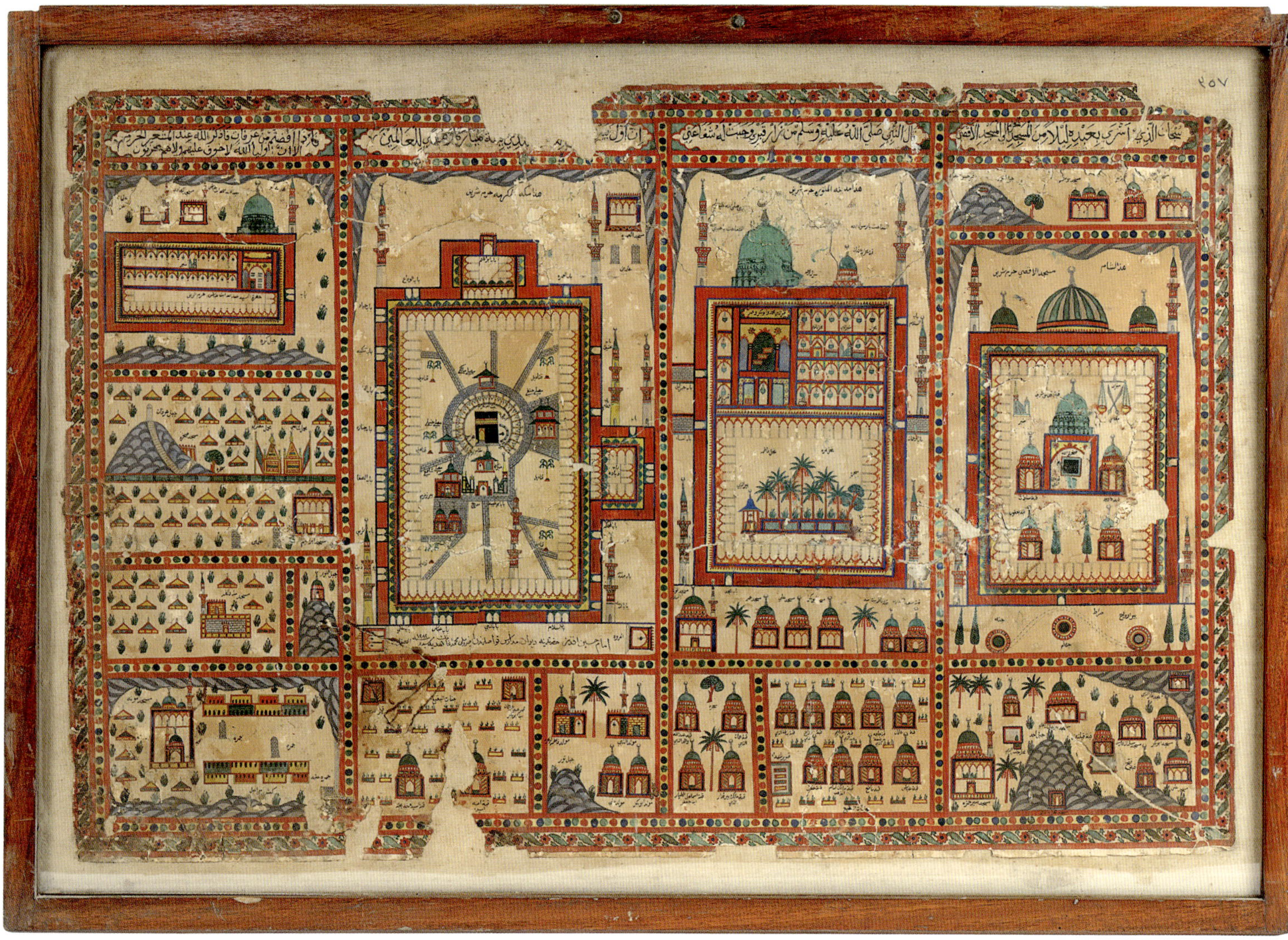

4.6 **Painting of the Three Holy Mosques**

In addition to depicting the three holiest mosques of Islam – Makkah, Medina and Jerusalem – there are other unidentified sites, including mosques and cities, on the left and bottom sides of the painting.

Egypt, 1865
Opaque watercolor on paper
Length: 69 cm, Width: 107 cm
Museum of Islamic Art, Cairo 357

4.7 **Manuscript of the Holy Qur'an**

This late Ottoman-era copy of the Holy Qur'an is decorated with European baroque-style motifs and includes paintings of the Two Holy Mosques of Makkah and Medina.

Turkey, 1833
Painted and gilded paper with leather binding
Height: 18 cm, Width: 11 cm
Museum of Islamic Art, Cairo 18104

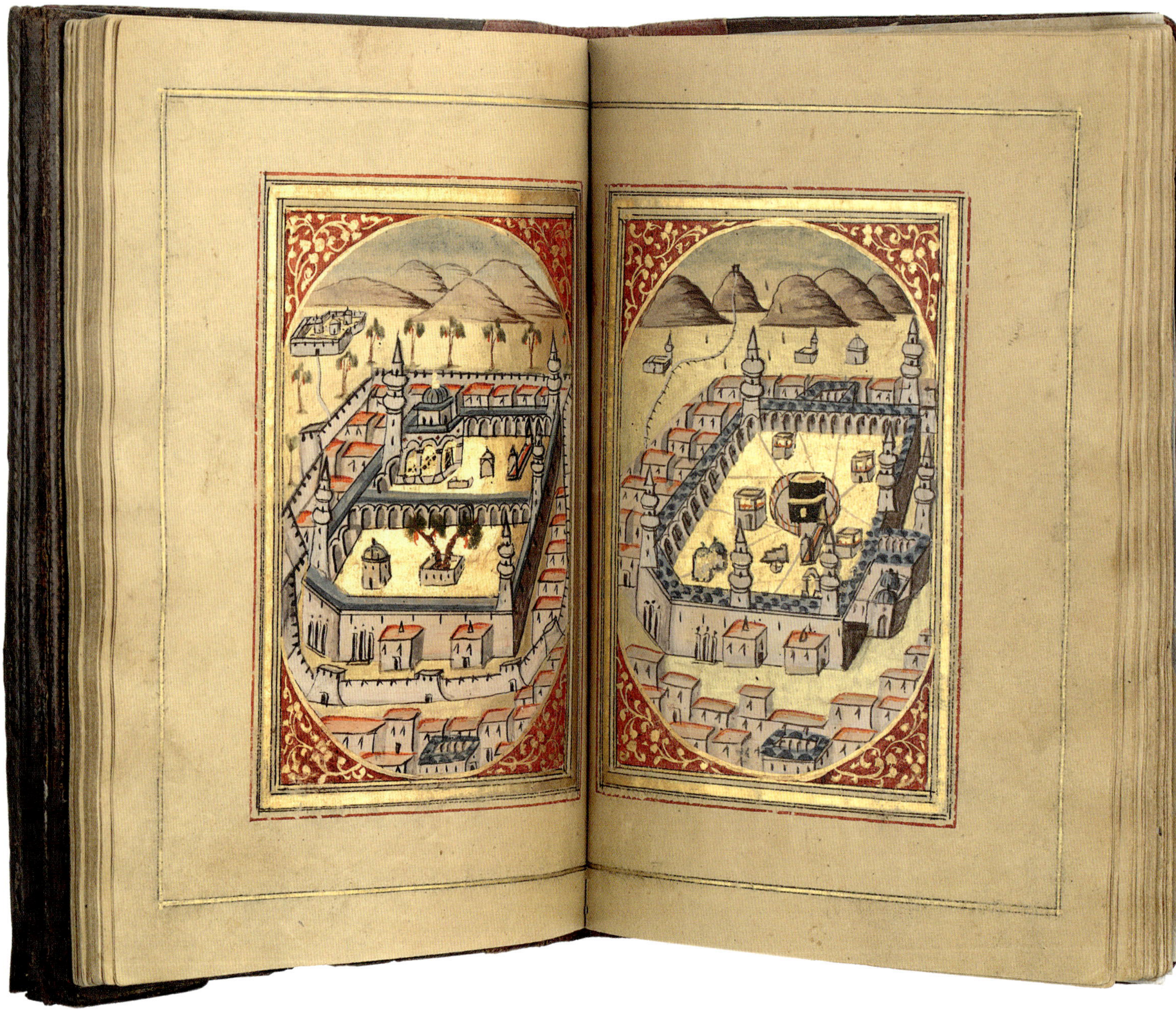

4.8 **Manuscript of the *Dala'il al-Khayrat***
Painted by Ismael Al-Zohdi, this double-page spread shows the Holy Mosques of Makkah and Medina and is found in a copy of the *Dala'il al-Khayrat* (Waymarks of Benefits) by Al-Jazuli (d. 1465). Late 18th-century copies of the work, such as this one, tend to include perspective views of the two Holy Sanctuaries.

Turkey, 19th century
Painted and gilded paper with leather binding
Height: 23 cm, Width: 16 cm
Museum of Islamic Art, Cairo 18170

4.9 **A Handbook for Hajj Pilgrims**
This topographical depiction of the Masjid al-Haram (Makkah) is found in a manuscript of the Futuh al-Haramayn (Revelations of the Two Holy Sites) by Muhyi al-Lari (d. 1526). It was copied by Muhammad Zarif of Rajastan, India, and was used as a guide for Hajj pilgrims to illustrate and describe the stations of the pilgrimage and the rituals.

India, Rajasthan, the village of Sojat
Painted and gilded paper
Dated Ramadan 1793
Height: 21.7 cm, Width: 13.6 cm
Ithra Museum 2020.0066

لا أنها تعطل من الحروب جميع حسبن إذ البيان أعظم إلا المقاتل وأصلها والتخصيص مقاده فالقتل والإثخان في القوم أن يكثر فيهم القتلى
والجرحى والمعنى فشدوا الوثاق بمن لم يقتل ولم يترتب فيه إلا الأسر ومنا وفداء مصدران منصوبان بفعلين مضمرين وقرأ جمهور الناس فداء
وقرأ ابن عامر في رواية كثير عنه فدى مقصور وإمام المسلمين مخير في الأسارى في خمسة أوجه القتل أو الاسترقاق أو ضرب الجزية أو الفداء أو المن ويحتج
في أسير أسير بحسب حاله من النكاية في المسلمين أو ضد ذلك وقوله تعالى حتى تضع الحرب أوزارها معناه حتى تذهب وتزول أثقالها و
والأوزار الأثقال ومنه قول الشاعر عمرو بن معديكرب الزبيدي : وأعددت للحرب أوزارها رماحا طوالا وخيلا ذكورا
وقال الثعلبي وغيره أوزارها في هذه الآية الآثام جمع وزر أي حتى تضع الحرب آثامها أن يكون فيها آثام في أحد الجانبين وأهل الملة ولو في
الله عنها تضع الحرب أوزارها وقال قتادة حتى يسلم الجميع فتضع الحرب أوزارها وقال أهل الكلام حتى تغلبوهم
وتقتلوهم وقال مجاهد حتى ينزل عيسى ابن مريم عليه السلام قال القاضي أبو محمد وظاهر اللفظ أنها استعارة يراد بها التزام الأمر أبدا وذلك
أن الحرب بين المومنين والكافرين لا تضع أوزارها فجاء هذا كما تقول أفعل كذا وكذا إلى يوم القيامة فإنما تريد أنك تفعله دائما وقوله تعالى ذلك تقدير
الأمر ذلك ثم قال ولو يشاء الله لانتصر منهم أي بعذاب من عنده يهلكهم به في حين واحد لكنه تعالى أراد اختبار المومنين وأن يبلو
بعض الناس ببعض وقرأ جمهور الناس قاتلوا وقرأ عاصم الجحدري بخلاف عنه قتلوا بفتح القاف والتاء وقرأ أبو عمرو وحفص عن عاصم والأعرج
والأعمش قتلوا بضم القاف وكسر التاء وقرأ زيد بن ثابت والحسن والجحدري وعيسى وأبو رجاء قتلوا بضم القاف وشد التاء وكسرها
وتأويل الجميع واحد معنى وقال قتادة نزلت هذه الآية فيمن قتل يوم أحد من المومنين وقوله تعالى سيهديهم أي إلى طريق الجنة وقوله
في إصلاح البال وروي عن عباس بن المفضل عن أبي عمرو ويدخلهم بسكون اللام وفي الدعاء منهم يجمعكم وفي سورة الإنسان إنما
يسكون العين والميم فيها وقوله تعالى عرفها لهم قال أبو سعيد الخدري وقتادة ومجاهد معناه بينها لهم أي جعلهم يعرفون منازلهم
فيها وفي نحو هذا المعنى قول النبي صلى الله عليه وسلم لأحدكم بمنزله في الجنة أعرف منه بمنزله في الدنيا وقالت فرقة معناه سماها
ورسمها كل منزل باسم صاحبه فهذا نحو من التعريف وقالت فرقة معناه طيبها لهم ومنها وعلاها وهذا من لا عرف الذي في الغيلان وما
يشبهها ومنه أعراف الخيل وقال مورج وغيره معناه طيبها مأخوذ من العرف ومنه طعام معرف أي مطيب وعرفت القدر طيبتها بالملح
وقوله تعالى إن تنصروا الله ينصركم حذف مضاف أي دين الله ورسوله والمعنى بنصره نحوكم وإنما عكم وإياكم ينصركم الله بخلق القوة
والجراءة وغير ذلك من المعاون وقرأ جمهور الناس ويثبت بالفتح الثاء المثلثة وشد الباء وقرأ المفضل عن عاصم ويثبت بسكون الثاء
وتخفيف الباء وهذا التثبيت هو في مواطن الحرب على الإسلام وقيل على الصراط في القيامة وقوله تعالى فتعسا لهم معناه عثارا وهلاكا
وسوء لهم وهو دعاء للعاثر إذا دعي له بالنش ومنه قول الشاعر : ماسين إن عثرت حتى يقيد ولا دعا لا ولا دعا تعسا
وقال الأعشى : بذات لوث عفرناة إذا عثرت فالتعس أدنى لها من أن أقول لعا
ومنه قول أم مسطح لما عثرت في مرطها تعس مسطح قال ابن السكيت التعس أن يخر على وجهه والنكس أن يخر على رأسه وتعسا مصدر نصبه فعل مضمر وقوله تعالى كرهوا ما أنزل الله يريد القرآن وقوله تعالى فأحبط
أعمالهم يقتضي أن أعمالهم التي في كفرهم لهم فيها بعض محبوطة قال القاضي أبو محمد رضي الله عنه ولا خلاف أن الكافر له
يكتبون حسناته وأحباط الناس في حسناتهم وقالت فرقة سو يلقاه بها يوم علينا ينعم الدنيا فيك وقالت فرقة هي محاه من أجل ثواب
ومن أجل أنه يسلم فيطرح ذلك إلى حسناته في الإسلام وهذا أحرى وبين في قول النبي صلى الله عليه وسلم لحكيم بن حزام أسلمت على
ما سلف لك من خير فعوقبوا قالوا ما وليه أسلمت على أن نعود ذلك ما سلف من خير وهذا هو الثاني وقيل الزيف أمر الله وقالت فرقة معناه أسلمت على إسقاط
ما سلف لك من خير إذ ينوب عليه نعم دنياك وذكر الطبري أن أعمالهم لنفي في هذه الآية محبطها في عبادتهم الأصنام وكفرهم ونفي
جعلها من أعمال الخير لا يذكو ولا يعتد به لذلك كالزبد أحبط قوله تعالى
أفلم يسيروا في الأرض فينظروا كيف كان عاقبة الذين من قبلهم دمر الله
عليهم وللكافرين أمثالها ذلك بأن الله مولى الذين آمنوا وأن الكافرين لا مولى لهم
إن الله يدخل الذين آمنوا وعملوا الصالحات جنات تجري من تحتها الأنهار والذين كفروا
يتمتعون ويأكلون كما تأكل الأنعام والنار مثوى لهم وكأين من قرية هي
أشد قوة من قريتك التي أخرجتك أهلكناهم فلا ناصر لهم ∴ قوله تعالى أفلم يسيروا توقيف لقريش
والذين من سلفهم بمن هلكوه وقوم لوط وقوم شعيب وأهل الشر وغيرهم والديار التي تسال ويوم الدار واحد من العراق وقوله دمر الله
عليهم ذلك والضمير في قوله أمثالها يصح أن يعود على العاقبة المذكورة ويصح أن يعود على الفعلة التي يتضمنها قوله دمر الله عليهم وقوله
ذلك ابتداء وخبر في أن وما عملت فيه والمولى الناصر الموالي وفي مصحف عبد الله بن مسعود ذلك بأن الله ولي الذين آمنوا وقال قتادة

5 The Wooden Tablet: The Transmission of Knowledge in the Mosque

Idries Trevathan

On a recent trip to the city of Fez in Morocco, I had the good fortune to visit the al-Qarawiyyin Mosque on several occasions. On each visit, following the prayers, I would sit to one side and observe the comings and goings of teachers and students as they went about their daily classes. I noticed how the teacher would seat himself on the floor of the mosque, leaning against a column, or sat on a raised seat against a wall with his pupils gathered in a circle (*halaqa*) around him. From a short distance away, I was able to hear the murmur of their voices and follow the gentle exchange between teacher and pupil. The class was conducted with the teacher prompting his students to read sections of the particular book they were studying, then periodically interrupt to ask a question on a particular point of interpretation, or to explain a difficult point. It was clear from their interaction that, while the teacher seemed to exercise authority, the students were allowed, in fact encouraged, to discuss and even challenge the teacher on certain points. Then, after an hour, these classes would end with the students rising, with their books in hand, slowly making their way out from the cool dimness into the mosque's bright courtyard (shown in Figure 5.1).

The profound significance of this routine was not lost on me. I was well aware that I was witnessing a tradition that has been unchanged from when al-Qarawiyyin was first established over 1,000 years ago. Indeed, according to UNESCO, the al-Qarawiyyin Mosque is the oldest existing, continually operating higher educational institution in the world. The al-Qarawiyyin is no exception and there are numerous other mosque universities that rank among the oldest surviving degree-granting institutes. These include the world-famous Al-Azhar in Cairo (Figure 5.2) which was founded in 970 and still serves as the world's preeminent center for Arabic literature and Sunni Islamic learning. These universities, as well as the school attached to the Prophet's Mosque in Medina, served as a model for future universities in the West, and contributed to an era of brilliance in learning.

← Detail of 5.19

Mosque and madrasa

It is difficult to overstate the historical importance of the mosque institution and its role in supporting literacy and education in local communities. During the first few centuries of the Islamic era, almost all higher and elementary education took place in the mosque and was based on religious sciences and related philological disciplines. However, according to the scholar Makdisi, after the mid-ninth century, many mosques also began to teach the legal sciences, as well as scientific subjects, including astronomy and engineering, along with courses on grammar, rhetoric, logic, elements of mathematics and astronomy (Makdisi. 1988, 65). In some mosques, even history, geography and elements of chemistry were also taught (Le Tourneau. 1961, 122). To give specific examples, the Qayrawan and Zaytuna Mosques in Tunisia were known to have taught the Holy Qur'an alongside jurisprudence, grammar, mathematics, astronomy and medicine (Djait. 1972, 378), whereas al-Qarawiyyin in Fez provided classes in medicine (Encyclopedia of Islam. 1971, 29–30). In one historic account by the famous Muslim traveler-geographer al-Muqaddasi (from Jerusalem), the 'Amr Mosque in Fustat, Egypt, was filled with students between the two evening prayers, studying law, the Qur'an, literature and wisdom (Tritton. 1957, 100). At the same time, in the eastern Islamic

5.1 **The Courtyard of the al-Qarawiyyin Mosque in Fez, Morocco**
Considered one of the world's oldest existing, continually operating higher educational institutions, al-Qarawiyyin continues to provide an excellent education in various disciplines to this day.

lands, courses in pharmacology, engineering and astronomy were taught in Baghdad mosques (Al-Khuli. 1987, 30).

Education within mosques was normally supported by generous endowments, or *waqfs*. Indeed, so considerable was the financial assistance through the *waqf* system that on his visit to the Great Mosque in Damascus, the 12th-century traveler Ibn Jubayr declared: "Anyone in the West who seeks success, let him come to this city (Damascus) to study, because assistance here is abundant. The chief thing is that the student here is relieved of all worry about food and lodging, which is a great help" (Totah. 1926, 45). Likewise, in the western Islamic lands, the scholar Makdisi wrote that students attending the Qarawiyyin in Fez were not only excused from paying fees, but were also given financial support to help with living expenses (Makdisi. 1998, 65). This support resulted in the mosque becoming a foundational and key factor in the spread of learning and knowledge and led to the cultivation of some of the most formidable scholars of any age including Ibn al-Haytham (d. 1040), Ibn Rushd (d. 1198), Ibn Khaldun (d. 1406), Ibn Harazim (d. 1235) and Ibn al-Khatib (d. 1374).

Thus, within a few centuries of the establishment of Islam, mosques in various Islamic capitals developed into prestigious places of learning, often with hundreds, sometimes thousands of students attending classes.

5.2 **Students Seated in the Courtyard of the Al-Azhar Mosque, Cairo, Egypt**
Much like today, this black-and-white photograph dating from the early 1880s shows students sitting in study circles (*halaqa*) in the courtyard of the university mosque of Al-Azhar.

On his visit to Damascus in the 14th century, Ibn Battuta recorded that more than 500 students were attending the study circles, or *halaqa*, of the great Umayyad Mosque (Totah. 1926, 45). Another scholar estimated that in the ninth century, the Great Mosque of Cordoba was enrolling around 4,000 students, with the total number in attendance reaching almost 11,000 (Scott. 1904, 465). Many of these students came from distant lands and would often stay and sleep in the very mosques where they attended lectures during the daytime. Some mature students or scholars might even make the mosque their home for many years, as for example the great theologian Al-Ghazali who was known to have lived in one of the minarets of the great Umayyad Mosque in Damascus. However, a mosque was not a suitable place for professors or a large number of students to live for long periods of time, so by the 11th century, schools, or madrasas, were being built adjacent to mosques to provide classrooms and accommodation. The model for the madrasa, like the mosque, can be seen to follow the Prophet's house in Medina (see Angawi in Chapter 2), or more accurately its courtyard that was adapted for the needs of the school. The typical madrasa plan was cruciform in plan, with four arched openings off the central courtyard. Student accommodation was normally arranged around the courtyard on two levels. The first great phase of madrasa construction occurred in the 11th century in the Seljuk Empire and is associated with the name of the great minister Nizam al-Mulk, who founded a number of madrasas known as *nizamiyyas*, the most important of which, the *nizamiyya* in Baghdad, became one of the greatest educational institutions in the Islamic world.

Books and libraries

Such learning would not have been possible or could have flourished without the mosque providing its students with access to books. The larger mosques frequently built important libraries and actively collected and copied books on different subjects, not only religious topics, but also those covering other types of scholarship. Some of these mosque libraries became the biggest repositories of books anywhere in the world. The Sayfiyya library – attached to the great Umayyad Mosque of Aleppo – reportedly had over 10,000 volumes and the Al-Azhar in Cairo and Cordoba Mosque library housed approximately 120,000 and 600,000 books respectively (Hassan. 2012, 77–8). Naturally, a large portion of these library holdings would include manuscripts of the Holy Qur'an for general use in the

5.3 **The Al-Attarine Madrasa, Fez, Morocco**
The courtyard of the Al-Attarine Madrasa in Fez, Morocco, located near the al-Qarawiyyin Mosque. It was built by the Marinid Sultan Uthman II Abu Said in 1323 and helped establish Fez as a center of learning and knowledge in the Islamic world.

mosque itself. Some of these manuscripts were specially commissioned for the mosque or donated following the death of a wealthy patron. In all cases, the manuscript would come under the care of the mosque's perpetual endowment, known as the *waqf*, which paid for the book's care and preservation. According to the *waqfiyya* (endowment deed) of the Qayrawan Mosque in Tunisia, the volume now known as the Blue Qur'an (shown in Figure 5.4) was donated sometime in the 13th century. While the *waqfiyya* does not specify the manuscript's exact origin, date and patronage, it is generally believed that the Blue Qur'an was produced in North Africa or Spain sometime in the late ninth to mid-10th century. Moreover, due to the lavish use of expensive gold calligraphy and indigo-dyed parchment, most scholars believe that it was probably commissioned by a caliph or a wealthy patron. As such, the use of this precious manuscript of the Holy Qur'an was probably restricted to ceremonial purposes in large congregational mosques by readers who had memorized the Holy Qur'an (due to the difficultly in reading the script). It was probably stored in the library and brought out and displayed in the mosque only during the holy month of Ramadan or during 'Id festivals and this partly explains its excellent state of preservation.

These mosque libraries often employed teams of professional scribes to copy books, including copies of the Holy Qur'an. It was not uncommon for aspiring calligraphers to receive their basic training within the same mosque where they had received their primary education. For example, according to the Mamluk *waqf* of the al-Ghuri Mosque complex in Cairo, a monthly sum of money of 300 dirhams was allocated for the *mu'allim al-khat* or calligraphy tutor to teach students, many of whom were orphans and had grown up in the mosque complex, the art of beautiful writing. Even today, this tradition continues and many mosques around the world offer classes in calligraphy as part of a child's basic education. As a case in point, the famous Saudi calligrapher and artist Nasser Al-Salem trained in traditional Qur'anic calligraphy within the Great Mosque of Makkah.

5.4 **Page from a Manuscript of the Holy Qur'an: Surat an-Nisa (4): 2–8**
According to the *waqfiyya* (endowment deed) of the Qayrawan Mosque in Tunisia, the volume from which this page comes – the Blue Qur'an – was donated to the mosque sometime in the 13th century.

Tunisia, probably Qayrawan, late ninth–early 10th century
Gold leaf, silver, and ink on parchment colored with indigo
Height: 28 cm, Width: 36 cm
Ithra Museum 2011.20.0001

The wooden writing tablet

Typically, scribes and calligraphers of the Holy Qur'an received a traditional education within the mosque institution; the first stage of their education when they were young normally included the memorization of the Holy

Qur'an. A typical class took place either within the mosque proper or the attached madrasa and would involve a large group of children gathered around a *hafiz* (someone who had memorized the Holy Qur'an) reciting different sets of verses aloud, sometimes in unison and sometimes at a different pace, over and over again. Students would traditionally read from a wooden writing tablet, or *lawh*, both because it is more economical and because, prior to the modern age, there was a limited availability of paper before the development of industrial mass-production. The 19th-century wooden tablet from Morocco shown in Figure 5.6 is one such example and has verses from the Holy Qur'an written on both sides. It is difficult to overemphasize the importance of this unassuming object in terms of its impact on Islamic civilization since it represents the principal support for Qur'anic memorization, and the practice of literacy more generally, in the Islamic world. Even today, the tradition of using the *lawh* thrives in many countries in North and West Africa. Indeed, so ubiquitous is the *lawh* in places like Mali and Nigeria that in many instances it has become a symbol of Islamic literacy and Qur'anic scholarship in itself. For example, in West Africa, the image of the *lawh* can be found on the walls of mosques, madrasas or the houses of teachers of the Holy Qur'an (see Figure 5.5).

5.5 **The Grand Mosque of Mopti, Mali**
A young boy on the way to Qur'an class at the Grand Mosque of Mopti, Mali. Verses of the Holy Qur'an can be seen written on the wooden board (*lawh*) he is carrying under his arm.

The process of teaching children how to read and write the Holy Qur'an began with writing out certain formulas on the tablet that would be recited before reading from the Holy Qur'an. After they have learned to recite these formulas, the teacher then writes the *fatiha* (first Surah of the Holy Qur'an) on the tablet and the children follow suit, line by line, until they memorize it in its entirety. Following this, each pupil will then wash the ink off the tablet and proceed in the same way with the other chapters, going from the shorter chapters at the end of the Holy Qur'an to the longest ones at the beginning. Once a verse has been memorized, water is again used to wash the text off and the student starts again by writing a new verse. The water used to wash the boards was treated with appropriate reverence and, in some instances was consumed, as it was believed to be useful in helping ward off various afflictions. Finally, once the student had memorized the whole Holy Qur'an (or a large portion), as well as writing it on his wooden slate, a matriculation ceremony (*khatma*) would take place. The ceremony would involve a new graduate reciting sections of the Holy Qur'an to his teachers and a gathered audience, after which they were given a decorated writing wooden tablet like the one on which they had learned to write and read the Holy Qur'an (an example of a decorated tablet is shown in Figure 5.7).

بسم الله الرحمن الرحيم وصلى الله على سيدنا محمد وعلى آله وصحبه أجمعين
بسم الله الرحمن الرحيم والطور وكتاب مسطور في رق منشور والبيت
المعمور والسقف المرفوع والبحر المسجور إن عذاب ربك لواقع ما له من دافع
يوم تمور السماء مورا وتسير الجبال سيرا فويل يومئذ للمكذبين الذين هم في خوض
هم ينظرون وإن للذين ظلموا عذابا دون ذلك ولكن أكثرهم لا يعلمون
واصبر لحكم ربك فإنك بأعيننا وسبح بحمد ربك حين تقوم ومن الليل
فسبحه وإدبار النجوم صدق الله العظيم

5.6 **Writing Board, with Text from the Holy Qur'an: Surat al-Tur (52): 1–49**
Prior to the mass production of paper, mosques and madrasas taught the reading and writing of the Holy Qur'an by copying passages onto wooden boards, called *lawh*. Once verses were memorized, the writing was washed off and the student would begin anew by copying out new verses.

Morocco, Berber. 18th–19th century
Ink on wood
Height: 58.4 cm, Width: 36.2 cm
Ithra Museum 2019.0063

5.7 **Writing Board, with Text from the Holy Qur'an: Surat al-'Alaq (96): 1–14**
Having memorized the entire Holy Qur'an, the graduating students were allowed to keep the boards, from which they had learned to read and write. This is an example of a decorated board awarded at graduation.

Morocco, Berber, 18th–19th century
Ink on wood
Height: 47 cm, Width: 28 cm
Ithra Museum 2019.0064

Thus, these simple wooden writing tablets were not only an indispensable practical tool for the transmission of Qur'anic knowledge. Their widespread use in the context of the mosque or madrasa was largely responsible for high levels of literacy in the medieval Islamic world. Indeed, while it is difficult, if not impossible, to calculate literacy rates in premodern Muslim societies, many scholars are of the opinion that Muslim societies had much higher literacy rates compared to their European neighbors during the medieval period.

5.8 **Page from a Manuscript of the Holy Qur'an: Surat al-'Isra (17): 95–111**
The script used in this Qur'an page is in a style midway between the early Hijazi Qur'an leaves and the fully formed classic 'Abbasid Kufic Qur'ans of the ninth and 10th centuries.

Near East or North Africa, c. 750–800
Ink on parchment
Height: 22.7 cm, Width: 31 cm
Ithra Museum 2019.0059

Writing, scripts and substrates

Historically, some of the students that graduated from the mosque would go on to become scribes or even great calligraphers, dedicating their lives to producing beautiful copies of the holy book. These calligraphers focused upon copying the Holy Qur'an as a task of religious merit and aestheticism and diligently trained and specialized in the Arabic scripts that had developed ever since the Holy Qur'an was first written down by the companions of the Prophet (ﷺ) during the seventh century. Indeed,

5.9 **Page from a Manuscript of the Holy Qur'an: Surat al-Jinn (72): 23–25**
Like many early Qur'an manuscripts, this one is written on parchment in black ink with a broad-nib reed pen. The horizontally elongated letters seen here are typical of early Kufic script.

Made possibly in Syria,
late ninth–early 10th century
Ink and gold on parchment
Height: 23.5 cm, Length: 33.5 cm
Ithra Archive

according to tradition, the Holy Qur'an was collected together from fragments and written down as a single volume during the reign of Uthman ibn Affan (d. 656), the third of the Rightly Guided Caliphs. However, these early manuscripts had neither diacritical nor vocalization marks which meant that reading them was often challenging, especially for those whose first language was not Arabic or those who had not memorized the Holy Qur'an. As Islam spread and was embraced by other cultures and peoples, many of whom did not speak Arabic, it became critically important to make the text as clear and legible as possible. Very early on, diacritical marks were introduced to distinguish consonants and short vowels and vocalization was indicated by single or double oblique strokes. However, as demonstrated in the early folio shown in Figure 5.8, the use of diacritics and vocalization was not prevalent and it was only in the late 10th century, when Islam had been established in non-Arab lands, that it was used systematically. This folio is one of the earliest surviving fragments of the Holy Qur'an and dates to the middle of the eighth century. It is written on vellum leaves in a script that is similar to a slanting script known as "Hijazi," which references the area encapsulating Makkah and Medina from which Islam originates geographically. The characteristic features of Hijazi script include the slanted verticals which lean slightly to the right and its distinctive triangular upward return of the final forms of the letters *nun* and *lam*, as well as the final form of the letter *qaf* that drops in a deep hook to the line below.

It was during the Abbasid period (750–1258), with its capital in Baghdad, when calligraphy began to develop into a more sophisticated art form. Among the new scripts found in Holy Qur'an manuscripts dating from this period is a script known as "Kufic," named after the city of Kufa in Iraq. This comprises a horizontally elongated, angular and slow-moving script. Two instances of this script can be found in the Blue Qur'an (Figure 5.4), shown earlier, and Figure 5.9, both of which are excellent examples of this dignified and monumental script. Later, other types of Kufic began to develop, including a floral Kufic, foliated Kufic, plaited or interlaced Kufic, bordered Kufic, and squared Kufic. In addition to western Kufic and eastern Kufic, the preeminence of the Kufic scripts encompasses a whole diversity of styles and was applied to a diversity of media.

By the late 11th century, the use of Kufic script for copying manuscripts of the Holy Qur'an was superseded (although it continued to be used as a decorative element in buildings, most notably the mosque) by an array of other cursive scripts. These were developed, in part, because of the need for more legible writing due to the vast number of non-Arabs adopting the religion. Baghdad became the center for the arts and famous Arab calligraphers such as Ibn al-Muqla and Ibn al-Bawwab worked on standardizing their new calligraphic scripts according to geometric principles and the proportions of the width of the calligrapher's reed pen. They developed what became known as the six "proportioned" cursive scripts: Naskh, Thulth, Muhaqqaq, Rayhan, Tawqi and Riqa. The development of these scripts was accompanied and affected by changes in the materials and tools of writing. For example, while paper was available from the eighth century, it did not supplant vellum in the production of the Holy Qur'an until the 11th century in the eastern Islamic lands and much later (14th century) in the western lands such as Morocco and Spain. For example, the manuscript shown in Figure 5.10 was written on vellum sometime in the 14th century, when paper had largely replaced vellum in central Islamic lands like Egypt, Syria and Iraq. This change from vellum to paper also followed a change from using a horizontal format instead of a vertical one.

5.10 **Page from a Manuscript of the Holy Qur'an: Surat al-Ma'ida (5): 29–31**
This Qur'an folio is written in Maghribi script, a style that was predominantly used in North Africa and Islamic Spain from the 11th century. It is written on parchment typical for Qur'ans from the region in the 13th and 14th centuries, even though paper was already being used throughout the rest of the Islamic world.

Andalusia or North Africa,
13th–14th century
Ink, opaque, watercolor and gold on parchment
Height: 22.8 cm, Width: 20 cm
Ithra Museum 2019.0047

فتكون من اصحب النار وذلك
جزؤا الظلمين فطو
عت له نفسه قتل اخيه فقتله
فاصبح من الخسرين فبعث
الله غرابا يبحث في الارض
ليريه كيف يوري سوءة اخيه
قال يويلتى اعجزت ان اكون مثل
هذا الغراب فاوري سوءة
اخي فاصبح من الندمين

عَلَيْهِ إِن كُنتُم بِآيَاتِهِ مُؤْمِنِينَ

وَمَا لَكُمْ أَلَّا تَأْكُلُوا مِمَّا

ذُكِرَ اسْمُ اللَّهِ عَلَيْهِ وَقَدْ

فَصَّلَ لَكُم مَّا حَرَّمَ عَلَيْكُمْ

إِلَّا مَا اضْطُرِرْتُمْ إِلَيْهِ وَإِنَّ كَثِيرًا

By the 13th and 14th centuries, new heights in calligraphic sophistication were reached under the Mongol (Ilkhanid) rule in Persia and the Near East (1256–1353) and some of the most beautiful Holy Qur'an manuscripts ever made were produced during this period. The large folio shown in Figure 5.11 is one such example. It originates from a manuscript of selected chapters from the Holy Qur'an known as the "Five Surahs" which begin with the phrase "AlhamduliIlah" (meaning "Thanks be to God" and found in Holy Qur'an chapters 1, 5, 18, 34 and 35). Each page has five lines of beautiful Muhaqqaq script outlined with brush-applied gold and rosettes marking the end of each verse. This piece was produced at the time when Mamluk rulers in Egypt were commissioning some of the most beautiful, and largest, copies of the Holy Qur'an ever created.

While the Mamluk and Ilkhanid manuscripts were similar in terms of their scripts and illumination, a completely separate calligraphic tradition was simultaneously being developed in western Islamic lands such as North Africa and Spain. For example, the folio shown in Figure 5.10 shows a manuscript of the Holy Qur'an written in what is called Maghribi script, which is a style of handwriting that was typical of copies from that region in the 13th and 14th centuries, and is characterized by deep curves of the letters below the line.

5.11 Large Page from a Royal Manuscript of the Holy Qur'an: Surat al-An'am (6): 118 120
Written by the calligrapher Abu Muhammad al Tabrizi, this superbly measured and flowing Muhaqqaq script is remarkable because the letters are individually outlined in gold. The manuscript may have been commissioned by a member of the Jalayirid royal family, who reigned from 1356 to 1374 with their capital in Baghdad.

Baghdad, 1370
Paper, Ink, gold leaf
Height: 43.2 cm, Width: 35.8 cm
Ithra Museum 2019.0045

Another separate calligraphic tradition was also forming in China during this period. After the collapse of the Mongol Empire, production of Holy Qur'an manuscripts in China remained isolated from trends in the West, and continued to develop from the archaic Persian style that was popular in the pre- and early Mongol period. Isolation from Islamic lands to the West meant that Chinese Holy Qur'an manuscript production was remarkably conservative and changed little over the centuries. For example, only the condition and paper distinguish this 18th-century Holy Qur'an (Figure 5.12) from the earliest surviving Chinese Holy Qur'an manuscripts which date back to 1401.

Under the Timurid dynasty, which ruled Persia from the late 14th to early 16th centuries, calligraphy underwent some major developments, such as the introduction of the Nastaliq script, which is still extensively used in the region today. Even after their collapse, the Timurid calligraphic tradition inspired all three major Islamic dynasties that ruled Muslim lands from the 16th century onwards – the Ottomans, the Mughals and the Safavids.

Final remarks

The Holy Qur'an folios shown here are just some examples from a writing tradition that spans 1,000 years and were produced in places as far apart as Spain and China. Many of these manuscripts had pride of place in mosque libraries and were copied by scribes and calligraphers who received their education and training within the mosques where they worked. Indeed, this intimate connection between learning to read and write the Holy Qur'an, literacy and general learning and knowledge as taught in the mosque, shows us that Islamic religion and knowledge went together, closely, and from the very early stages. Other than the Holy Qur'an and Hadith (the sayings of the Prophet Mohammed (ﷺ), the concrete symbol of Islam has to be the mosque, for it was the center of learning and knowledge for one of the greatest and most learned religious civilizations the world has ever known. Indeed, in most parts of the Islamic world, the Arabic word *Jama'a* has meant both mosque and school. Similarly, the Arabic word for university, *Jami'a*, derives from *Jama'a* (mosque). There are few, if any, similar derivations in other languages or cultures linking education and worship so fundamentally. There can be few better examples of the intimate link between mosque and learning.

5.12 **Manuscript of the Holy Qur'an in 30 Volumes**
Possibly housed in a mosque hall or library, this complete set of 30 volumes of the Holy Qur'an is in excellent condition and may have only been used on special occasions such as during Ramadan.

China, 18th century
Ink on paper
Height: 24.8 cm, Width: 18.4 cm
Ithra Museum 2019.0010.1-30 to 2019.0010.30-30

5.13 **Qur'an Box**

Originally housed in Cairo's Umm al-Sultan Sha'ban Mosque madrasa, the interior of this box is divided into three compartments of 10 slots, each of which would have contained one volume of a 30-part edition of the Holy Qur'an.

Cairo, Egypt, 1369
Wood, inlaid with ivory, ebony and tin
Length: 41 cm, Height: 28 cm, Diameter: 71 cm
Museum of Islamic Art, Cairo. 452

5.14 **Manuscript of the Holy Qur'an**
This late Ottoman Qur'an from Egypt shows the classic illuminated treatment in gold and blue of the opening two pages of the Holy Qur'an, including Surat al-Fatiha (the Opening) and Surat al-Baqara (the Cow).

Egypt, 1590
Ink, opaque watercolor and gold on paper
Length: 21.5 cm, Width: 13 cm
Museum of Islamic Art, Cairo 18150

5.15 **Manuscript of the Holy Qur'an**

With its beautifully illuminated and gold gilt frontispiece, this manuscript of the Holy Qur'an is a splendid example of lavish manuscript production in the late Ottoman period.

Egypt, 1872
Ink, opaque watercolor and gold on paper
Length: 12.5 cm, Width: 8.5 cm
Museum of Islamic Art, Cairo 18081

5.16 **Manuscript of the Holy Qur'an**
Considering its excellent state of preservation, this 19th-century manuscript of the Holy Qur'an may have been in the care of a mosque *waqf* which oversaw its care and conservation.

Egypt, 1872
Ink, opaque watercolor and gold on paper
Length: 19.5 cm, Width: 13 cm
Museum of Islamic Art, Cairo 18050

5.17 **Miniature Manuscript of the Holy Qur'an**

Such miniature Qur'ans are known by the term *sanjak*, which comes from the Turkish term now written as *sançak* and meaning "banner." This came from the practice among military standard-bearers of attaching the tiny texts to their flags. Travelers also wore them around their necks.

Egypt, 18th century
Ink, opaque watercolor and gold on paper
Diameter: 6 cm
Museum of Islamic Art, Cairo 18190

Enlarged detail

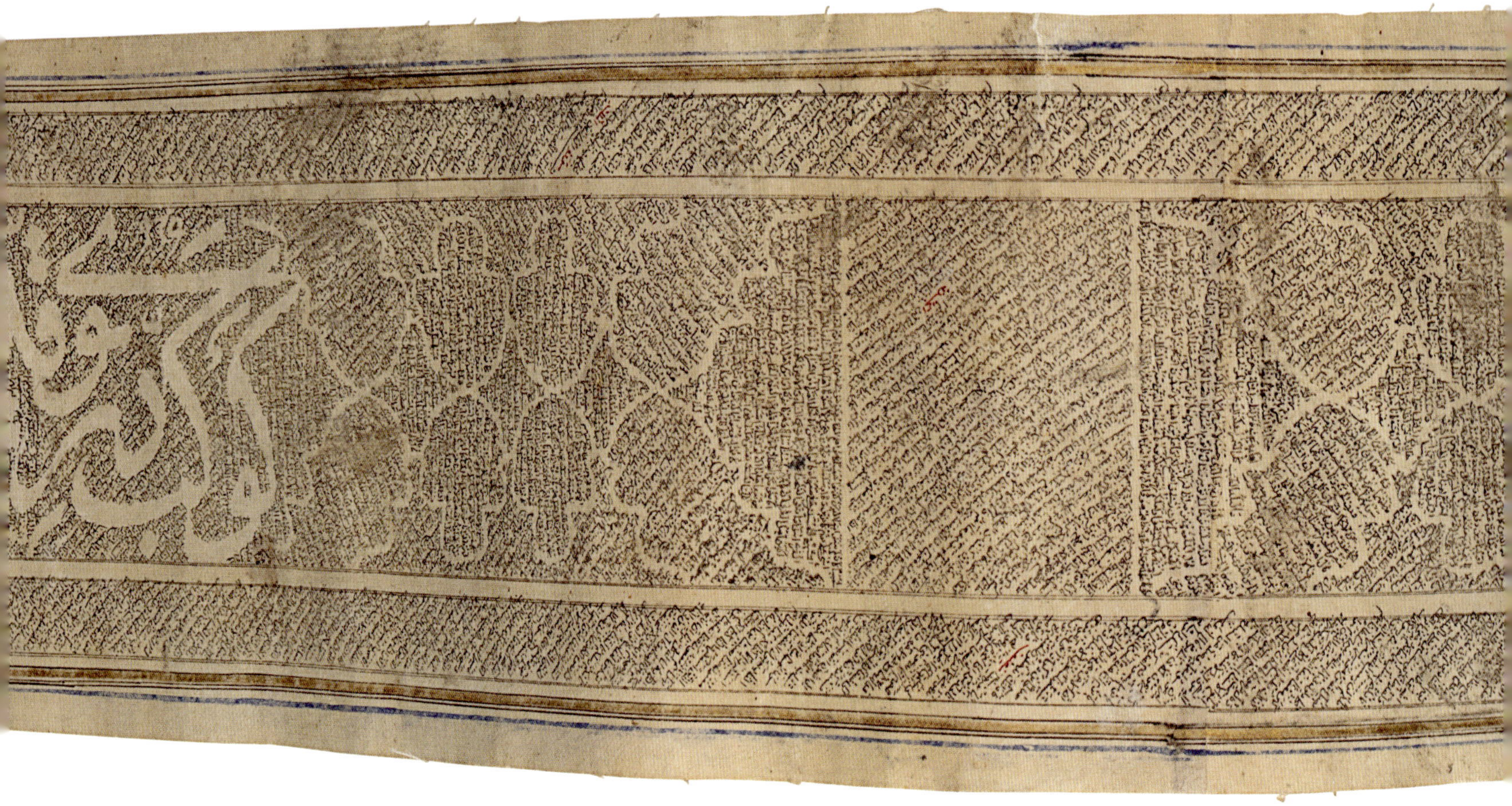

5.18 **Holy Qur'an in Scroll Format**

Written in minute black Ghubari script, this rare and fragile scroll manuscript contains the entire content of the Holy Qur'an.

Egypt, 18th century
Ink on paper
Length: 420 cm, Width: 8 cm
Museum of Islamic Art, Cairo 18131

5.19 **Book on Tafsir (A Commentary on the Holy Qur'an)**

Books on tafsir, such as the example shown here, were commonly found in mosque libraries. Written by the Andalusian scholar 'Abd al-Haqq ibn Abu Bakr al-Muharibi al-Garnati, known more commonly as Ibn 'Atiyyah (born in Granada in 1088), this book is considered his finest achievement and regarded by the scholar Ibn Taimiyya as one of the most reliable Qur'anic commentaries.

Andalusia, Spain, second half of the 12th century
Ink on paper with leather binding
Height: 27.3 cm, Width: 18.3 cm
Ithra Museum 2020.0067

5.20 **Book on Logic**

Historically, mosque libraries housed a range of books on diverse subjects. It would not be uncommon to find important textbooks like this *Matali' al-Anwar* (Sources of Light) by Al-Urmawi (d. 1283) on the topic of logic and physics. According to an inscription on the inside cover, the book was declared a *waqf* in 1527.

Mamluk provinces, possibly Iraq or Turkey, 1455
Paper and ink
Height: 27.3 cm, Width: 18.3 cm
Ithra Museum 2019.0046

5.21 **Pen Case**

This pen case is inlaid with silver and decorated with Thulth inscriptions. Such an item would have been used by an important calligrapher who was tasked with writing the Qur'an or important government documents, such as a mosque *waqfiyya* (mosque endowment deed).

Egypt, 15th century
Brass and silver
Depth: 9.5 cm, Length: 31 cm
Museum of Islamic Art, Cairo. 15934

5.22 **Pen Case**
A pen case comprising two separate tubular pen holders, and a cylindrical inkwell with a dome that shows obvious architectural influence from mosque design. Such a pen box could have been used by a wandering scribe or a student of calligraphy, with the case being slipped under the belt.

Northern India, 18th–19th century
Brass
Length: 26 cm, Height: 15 cm
Ithra Museum
2019.0053.1-4 to 2019.0053.4-4

5.23 **Pen Case**

The pen case unscrews to reveal a tube in which quills or reed pens were stored. Next to it is an inkpot and a sander, used to sprinkle sand on the written word to help it to dry without smudging.

Turkey, c. 1850
Brass and gold
Length: 25.5 cm, Diameter: 3.2 cm
Ithra Museum
2019.0058.1-5 to 2019.0058.5-5

5.24 **Calligrapher's Certificate**
According to Islamic tradition, knowledge of calligraphy was passed from teacher to student. After completing these studies successfully, a student receives a document called an *ijaza* (permission), shown here, enrolling the novice in the ranks of professional calligraphers.

Turkey, 18th century
Ink on paper
Height: 28 cm, Width: 17.5 cm
Museum of Islamic Art, Cairo 18175

5.25 **Folding Qur'an Stand**
The normal method of reading the Qur'an was to sit cross-legged on the floor in front of a folding stand like this one, which bears an inscription praising the name of the famous Mamluk Sultan al-Ghuri.

Cairo, Egypt, 16th century
Wood
Height: 40 cm, Width: 30 cm (closed)
Museum of Islamic Art, Cairo. 4114

5.26 **Folding Qur'an Stand**

This wooden Qur'an stand, made from one piece of wood and ornamented with geometric designs of bone, mother-of-pearl, horn and tortoiseshell inlay, would have been commonplace in the great mosques and madrasas of the Ottoman world, particularly in Syria.

Turkey, 18th–19th century
Wood, bone, mother-of-pearl, horn and tortoiseshell
Height: 81.5 cm, Width: 27 cm wide (closed)
Ithra Museum 2019.0052

5.27 **Folding Qur'an Stand**

This Mughal Qur'an stand may have belonged to a wealthy or important patron. Its high level of craftsmanship is testament to the importance of its function, and also indicates that it may have been made in a Mughal royal workshop.

India, 17th–18th century
Wood, ivory, tortoiseshell, gold foil and mica
Height: 44.4 cm, Width: 22.4 cm (closed)
Ithra Museum 2019.0048

5.28 **Table**
This masterpiece of Islamic woodwork was originally placed in the madrasa of Umm al-Sultan Sha'ban in Cairo. While such tables had various functions, in the context of a madrasa, it was most commonly used to support the Holy Qur'an manuscript as it was read. For protection, the manuscript could also be stored inside the tall stand.

Cairo, Egypt, 1369
Wood, inlaid with ivory, bone, redwood and ebony
Height: 115 cm, Diameter: 54 cm
Museum of Islamic Art, Cairo. 449

5.29 **Table**
Perhaps referencing the mosques in which they were used, these six-sided tables feature architectural motifs, such as pillars and archways. It was probably used as a surface to place candles, incense burners and copies of the Holy Qur'an.

Egypt, 18th century
Wood
Height: 98 cm, Width: 43 cm
Museum of Islamic Art, Cairo. 443

6 The Alchemy of Creation: A Meditation on the Geometry of Ceramic Tiles

Lisa DeLong

There is a resonance between clay and the craftsman. Both find their origins in the earth; both are intentionally shaped over time for a higher purpose than their humble origins would suggest. Both can be transformed through a form of alchemy which changes their very nature.

Roughly 700 years ago, a craftsman dug raw clay out of the ground and started the long process to refine it. He first removed all organic detritus – sticks, leaves, roots – then picked out rocks and pebbles and began breaking up lumps. Water was then added to form a slurry. This soupy mud was next filtered until only the finest clay particles remained. With extensive washing and sieving, eventually a wet, versatile clay body remained, ready to be shaped for a purpose. To make tiles, all air bubbles must be kneaded out of the refined clay. Next it is shaped by hand into flat slabs. This work is difficult, full-bodied labor.

Some workers mix and apply glazes, while others oversee the firing of the kiln. Achieving different glaze colors involves complex chemistry; skilled ceramicists know exactly how to adjust their recipes for color, luminosity and opacity. They were some of humanity's first chemists as they observed how raw elements reacted with each other as they were combined under intense heat. Loading and firing kilns requires a deep knowledge of air and fire. Individual pieces must be carefully stacked so that they do not fuse together as clay body and glaze transform under intense heat. They morph from earth to a substance more akin to glass. Different fuels can change the firing results. Those working with a specific kiln for a long time will come to know all of its capacities and quirks.

Specialization, and a resulting division of labor, is a common feature of traditional craft workshops because it is integrated with how each new generation absorbs the knowledge of its predecessors. From early youth, each craftsman builds skill upon skill, led by a master intimately acquainted

← Detail of 6.1

with every aspect of the craft. This traditional apprenticeship structure is still part of the zillij workshops of Fez, as well as the kashi workshops of Iran and Pakistan.

Because of the apprenticeship structure in traditional craft workshops, know-how could accumulate and build on the work of previous generations. The art of ceramics has developed over millennia. While the specific structure of the master-apprentice system might vary from place to place, essentially, it was a life-long path. Through travel, artisans were exposed to local innovations and creative solutions. Trade, particularly along the Silk Road, brought other innovations into the workshop, as did the exchange of ideas that naturally occurred as part of the Hajj journey to Makkah. As a result, a great deal of beautiful artistry was developed: geometric tiles, both molded and chiseled, tiles cut into elaborate floral forms, tiles delicately painted with brushes.

The "secrets" of a traditional workshop are not so much in the glaze recipes and the knowledge of how to construct complex geometric patterns, but in the relationships amongst the craftsmen and the knowledge that can only be communicated via careful observation and diligent practice. Keith Critchlow and Paul Marchant observe that "the secret lies in the relationship between master and apprentice over many years – at least a quarter of a century or a generation" (Damluji. 1992, 212).

An alchemical transformation

Ceramic art elevates earth through fire. Fire fundamentally alters the nature of earth. Clay, dug out of the dark depths, reaches a crystalline perfection. It begins as a soft and watery substance, dissolvable and transient. It can be washed away by a river or a rainstorm, or broken apart in one's fingers. Yet through the application of carefully controlled fire, this crumbly, dull, weak material will be fundamentally transformed into colorful, crystalline beauty worthy of the most sacred spaces. Fire creates structure from pliable forms. It makes clay rigid, turning earth into a substance with the capacity to protect people from the elements. Fire also gives glazed tiles a gemstone quality. In its new form, it symbolically bridges earth and heaven.

6.1 **Panel of Star and Cross Tiles**
Possibly decorating a Seljuk-era mosque or madrasa, this tile revetment panel features straight-line geometry comprising 15 cross tiles, each covered with a cobalt blue glaze. They are arranged in alternation with 24 eight-pointed star tiles covered with an opaque turquoise (copper) glaze.

Kashan, Iran, late 13th or early 14th century
Ceramic with cobalt and copper glaze
Height: 72 cm, Width: 47 cm
Ithra Museum 2019.0039

In the case of these tiles from Iran (probably Kashan, 13th–early 14th century), the glazes are the colors of the sky – a thorough transformation of earth's clay to heaven (Figure 6.1). This color palette is found throughout Central and South Asia, where heavenly blues are juxtaposed against earthy brick reds. Today, kashi craftsmen in Pakistan still speak of the light and dark blue glazes as the colors of the day and night skies. Similar blues can be found throughout the buildings of the Islamic world – Samarkand, Multan, Isfahan, Istanbul. Chemically, the colors come from cobalt (dark blue) and copper (turquoise).

Circle and square

I have been deeply interested in geometry for almost as long as I can remember; this interest has permeated my own art practice (Figure 6.2).

The elegant and sophisticated geometry found throughout the Islamic lands holds a particular fascination for me. The study of geometry was a core part of my PhD which I began in 2001 at the Visual Islamic and Traditional Arts program in London. The School of Traditional Arts is now part of the Prince's Foundation; I have been fortunate to be part of their outreach team for almost 15 years. A central part of my work for the school is developing programs around the world to teach traditional skills, including the "language" of geometry.

Geometry is present in the art and architecture of all civilizations, perhaps most conspicuously in edifices built for worship. Its harmonies govern decorative elements and organize spaces of human activity, endowing art and architecture with sacred significance, and directing heart and mind to the Divine with its order. In *The Need for a Sacred Science*, Dr. S. H. Nasr writes,

> This order is, moreover, related to an incredible harmony which in the technically musical sense pervades the realms of nature from the stars to subatomic particles. The proportion of the parts of animals and plants, of crystal structures or of planetary movements, when studied geometrically from the point of view of traditional or Pythagorean mathematics, reveal the presence of a harmony pervading all orders of the universe. It is as if the whole cosmos were music congealed into the very substance of things, which not only have their existence according to the laws of harmony, but also move and live according to the laws of the cosmic dance. (Nasr. 1993, 120)

Meditation on the circle and its inherent expression of oneness can be considered the heart of Islamic geometric pattern. Circles are drawn with compasses, a tool which combines both rest (the fixed central point) and activity (the inscribing of the circle's circumference). This echoes the layout of sacred sites where a temple or shrine is the fixed point around which the rest of human activity is centered.

6.2 **For the Beauty of the Earth**
Gouache, graphite, and ink on paper.
Inspired by a panel found in
a madrasa, Isfahan.
Lisa DeLong, 2019

The circle is closely associated with wholeness as it is entirely self-contained and generated by movement around the navel of a single point. In cultures around the globe, the circle is considered a symbol of the Divine, the heavens, and all things celestial. In dome form, it even more explicitly represents the heavens. It is associated with eternity, completeness, truth, inclusion, governance and perfection. All points on the circumference exist in a unified relationship to the center. It is a perfect

expression of unity and wholeness. The circle operates as a limitation, an enclosure, a boundary and a protection.

The circle can also be considered the mother of the shapes. All the polygons are born from the circle and from these is derived a sophisticated geometric patterning developed to an exceptionally high standard throughout the Islamic world. Paired with the circle, the square with its four sides is often considered to be a symbol of earth. The Brethren of Purity, a group of Muslim philosophers based in 10th-century Baghdad, discussed the four-fold nature of the created world thus:

> God himself has made it such that the majority of things of Nature are grouped in four such as the four physical natures which are hot, cold, dry and moist; the four elements which are fire, air, water and earth; the four humors ... the four seasons ... the four cardinal directions ... [and] the four winds. (Nasr. 1993, 50)

Geometric principles are not only found in polygons decorating flat surfaces, but in architectural space. They regulate the proportions and volumes of architectural space. In architecture, the circle and square are manifested in three-dimensional form as the cube and the sphere. These two shapes do not meet comfortably without a transition; to set a dome on a square structure requires a geometric, architectural bridge. This transition is most commonly octagonal. The octagon with its eight sides thus symbolically mediates between heaven and earth. There is an architectural inevitability to the use of this shape as it allows the volume of the square base to beautifully support the realms of the heavenly sphere. It is structurally logical and aesthetically pleasing, as well as spiritually significant.

Very broadly speaking, the patterns used by artisans over the centuries to decorate both sacred and secular spaces in the Islamic world fall into three primary categories of geometric pattern defined by the numbers behind their symmetries: three, four and five. The threefold family includes hexagons and triangles, as well as a whole array of other shapes derived from these fundamental forms. This family can also include twelvefold designs. The fivefold family has reached particular heights of development in the hands of Muslim artists over the centuries, including an almost infinite array of patterns governed by the numbers five and ten and the proportions of the golden ratio. There are additional geometries which do not fall neatly into these categories but which are nonetheless beautiful expressions of essential principles. The fourfold family, of which our tile panel is a primary member, consists of shapes derived from the square.

Breath of the Compassionate

This specific pattern, composed of two perfectly tessellating shapes – an eight-pointed star and a four-armed cross, each with 16 equal sides – has in recent decades become associated with the name "The Breath of the Compassionate." This name was attached to it by Professor Keith Critchlow, but the pattern itself is ancient. The name was offered as a poetic expression of the pattern's underlying geometric principles, where it can be seen that it contains shapes which appear to "contract" and "expand" as the breath of life swells and deflates our lungs. Critchlow writes,

> In fact all Islamic patterns can rightly be seen as examples of the "Breath of the Compassionate" as they "contract" and "expand" rhythmically. However this particular pattern … is a particularly clear example of the principle of two sixteen-sided figures one expanding into an eight-pointed star, the other contracting into a cruciform – both with exactly the same number of equal encompassing lies. It is the "Breath of the Compassionate" that gives us not only the patterns of order, but the magnificent world that we live in. (Critchlow. 2002, 3)

The association of this name with this pattern seems to have passed into common parlance, particularly recently as social media have facilitated the exchange of geometric pattern construction techniques.

Geometry

There is a difference between copying the appearance of a pattern and being able to generate it from first principles. If only the appearance is mimicked, the principles quickly become lost, mistakes can easily creep in and can be transmitted quickly as copies of copies are made. This is easily overcome by learning to draw in the same way that the old masters would have drawn their patterns.

To more fully demonstrate the principles of this specimen pattern, the following diagrams illustrate some ways in which the design and some of its derivatives can be constructed using tools known to the traditional artist – the compass and straight edge. A circle is drawn with a pair of dividers or compasses. A fixed point at the center punctures a navel, while the active radius traces the circle (Figure 6.3).

The symbolic complement of the circle is the square. Drawing a square requires both the compasses and a straight edge. The interaction of these two tools produces a shape with symmetries reflecting the patterns and cycles of earth: the four directions, four seasons, four elements, the four ages of humankind. These are echoed within both the symmetries of the human body and the architectural spaces we build to house the activities of our life.

1. A square is constructed first by drawing a circle centered on a horizontal line.

2. A perpendicular line through the circle's center is added, thus dividing the first circle into four, with intersections above, below, right, and left.

3. Four circles of the same radius centered at these intersections give rise to the intersections necessary to draw a square as indicated.

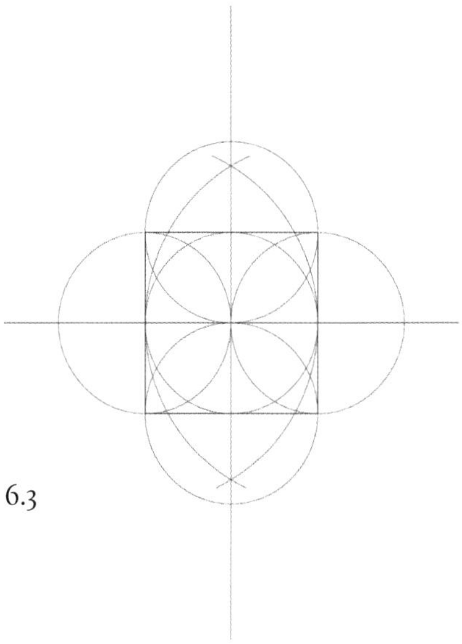

6.3

Squares are a symbol of earth, material form, and the created realms in many cultures. Leonardo da Vinci, following the writings of the Roman architect Vitruvius, noted that the human form could be represented as the embodiment of both circle and square: the circle centered at the navel circumscribing the outstretched arms and legs, a square drawn around them would designate both the height and the furthest expansion of the arms. Much the same way that a domed building might signify a place where heaven and earth might touch in the meeting of sphere and cube, the human body also expressed these bridging principles in the circle and square which define its proportions.

The turquoise star from the tile panel is formed by the overlapping of two squares to make an eight-pointed motif often known as the Seal of Solomon, or *khatim sulayman* (Figures 6.4 and 6.5).

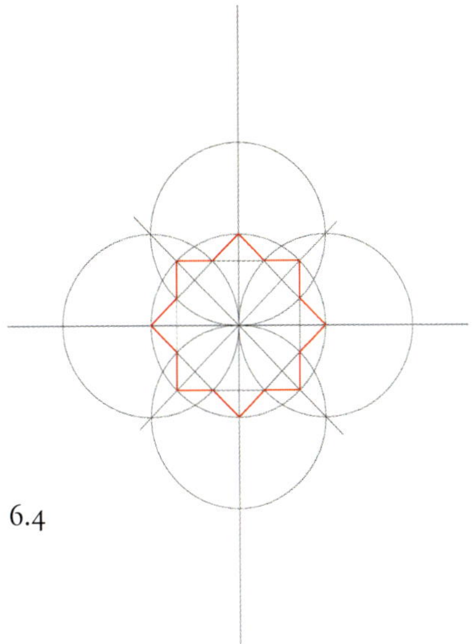

6.4

6.5

By adding diagonals to our square construction, the first circle we drew is now divided into eight.

These eight divisions can be used to inscribe two squares into that circle, thus giving rise to the khatim star.

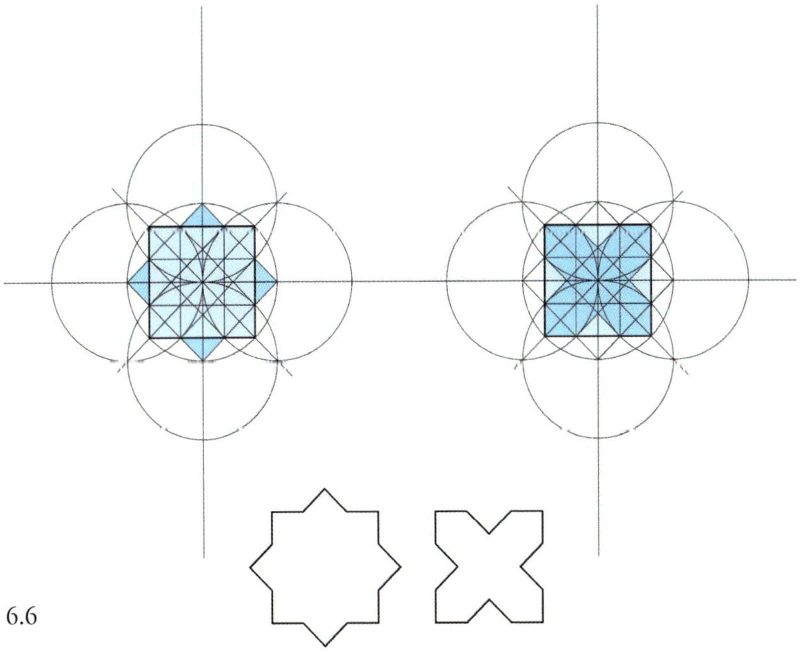

6.6

In the "Breath of the Compassionate" pattern, an expansion and contraction can be seen in the shapes themselves. Here, they are diagrammed as an expansion and contraction of a square (Figure 6.6).

A pattern of *khatams* touching point-to-point creates a new interstitial shape. In our tile panel, this secondary shape is a beautiful dark cobalt blue (Figure 6.7).

6.7

6.8

This "inhalation" and "exhalation" are a perfectly balanced complementarity. The shapes are mutually defining – they are each made possible by the existence of the other. The pattern can be extended infinitely across a plane (Figure 6.8).

This pattern has been a perennial source of inspiration to craft workshops. It can be considered one of the most fundamental patterns, not only for its ubiquity, but its versatility – its capacity to be developed into an infinite variety of forms from these mother shapes. Not only can the shapes themselves be painted with floral forms echoing the gardens of paradise or inscribed with the words of poetry and scripture, the internal principles can also be explored to give rise to an extended family of geometric masterpieces. Here is but one example from the Moroccan tradition of how a microcosm of geometric variation can be generated within the fundamental shapes of the basic pattern (Figures 6.9, 6.10).

Generations of masters throughout the Islamic lands have developed a fugue of complex patterns, all variations of these essential geometric qualities coaxed into expression from the proportions of the square. From a simple alphabet of two shapes, poetry in different geometric dialects has been composed throughout the Islamic world in many different media.

Contemporary inspiration

In this simple array of 39 tiles, we see more than an artifact miraculously preserved over many centuries. In them, we have a tangible trace of human skill dedicated to the purpose of beautification. We see earthy clay alchemically elevated to the crystalline heavens. It is unclear whether the tiles were made for a sacred or secular space, but we can tell that they were

6.9

6.10
Zillij tile decoration on the columns of Madrasa Bou Inania, Fez, Morocco. The ochre-colored tiles trace out a larger khatam shape with a lovely variation of an eightfold pattern in its interior.

created by masters who had knowledge and skill. These ancient masters' devotion to their medium is clearly evident in their craftsmanship. Their techniques were tested and refined by generations of artists before them, and they in turn set a standard for generations following them. This simple panel of tiles not only contains a potential which has been developed into an infinite range of patterns and crafts over the intervening centuries, but even now it continues to inspire artists. The tiles invite us to consider: "What do we make today that will survive to inspire artists centuries from now?" "What do we create that embodies a similar dedication to beauty and quality?"

Unfortunately, there has been a widespread decline in traditional crafts following industrialization. Inspired patrons are more difficult to find, as is a customer base that prizes skill and beauty more than it values the low cost through mass production. Traditional apprenticeship models and workshops have struggled to weather competition from industrialization and factory production. In addition to the loss of technical skills, knowledge of geometric design principles has also declined. Manufacturers of compasses, an essential tool for the designer, have ceased production.

Despite all this, we are seeing hints of a revival of traditional crafts. In recent years there has been a tremendous flowering of interest in learning to draw geometric patterns. Social media have connected communities of enthusiasts with one another, contributing to the dissemination and rediscovery of pattern construction following original principles and hand-drawn methods. Workshops and programs, such as those taught by the Prince's Foundation School of Traditional Arts in London, as well as individual teachers around the world, are part of a reawakening to the beauty of handmade crafts in a world dominated by plastic and mass production. Skills are being reintroduced to places where a line of tradition had been severed and reinvigorating places where traditions are barely surviving. In this way, these ancient ceramic tiles will not just be historical artifacts but represent living traditions.

In these simple blue and turquoise tiles, we see an art form bearing the traces of ancient alchemy that can be just as alive today as it was centuries ago. We can return to the original principles which inspired these tiles and make contemporary work that is truly *original* – work that is founded in original principles, rather than simply "different." In this way, our work can become part of a living tradition rather than copies of a dead past. Beautiful

6.11
The stunningly beautiful interior dome of Sheikh Lotfullah Mosque, Isfahan. At the very center of this dome is a small, turquoise, eight-petal shape which unfolds into a peacock-like array of shamsas. It is an elaborate floral expression of the same fundamental geometric principles as the eight-pointed star in the tiles from Kashan at the heart of this essay.

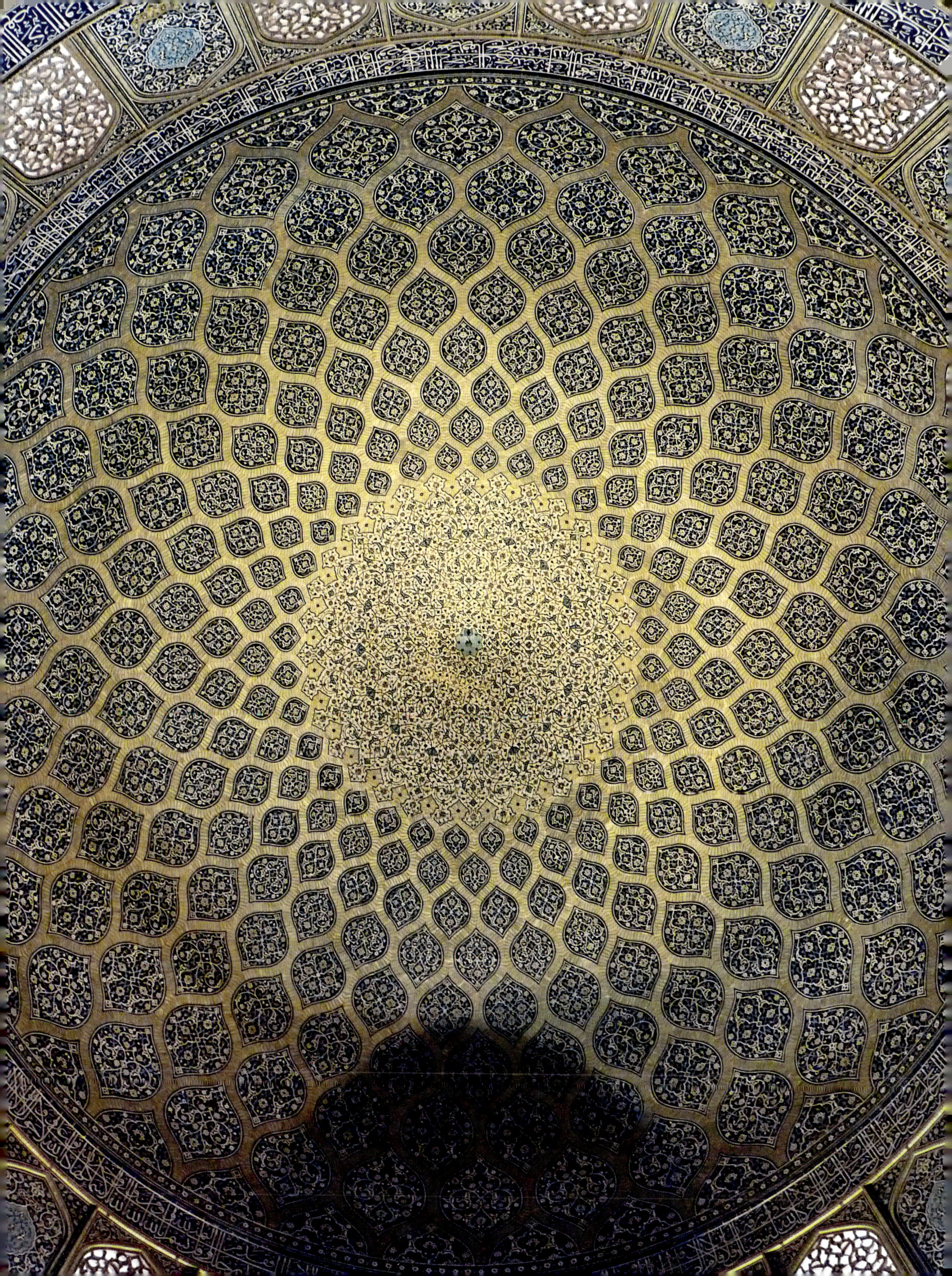

work inspired by devotion to the Origin of all has as much relevance today as it did centuries ago.

Beauty, worship and transformation

The original architectural context of these tiles is lost to history. However, whether a building is domestic or public, secular or sacred, functional or inspiring (and it might very well be many of these simultaneously), the adornment of its surfaces cannot help but influence the human beings who move through its spaces.

In its best manifestations, a building and its ornamentation will elevate, protect, inspire, uplift and support human beings in the rhythms of work and worship. A beautifully tiled mosque does all these thing by surrounding worshippers with forms and proportions that echo the principles of creation; they cannot help but profoundly affect the human being who prays there.

When a visitor enters a beautifully proportioned space, such as the Sultan Hassan Mosque in Cairo, the exquisitely domed Sheikh Lotfullah Mosque in Isfahan or the cosmically tiled vaults of Shah Jahan Mosque in Thattha, they are profoundly affected in ways that are difficult to articulate (Figures 6.11, 6.12). Fortresses of prayer, temples of devotion and monuments to beauty – these buildings reflect humanity's greatest aspirations, as well as profound humility before the Divine. In each place and time, the local artisans meditate on and interpret the principles of Islam in clay and brick and stone, reflecting both the particular and the universal.

A visitor to a mosque might first find their gaze raised to majestic dome, arcing across the heavens above, its geometry simultaneously crystallizing and dissolving physical space. The eye might then be caught by elements at the more humble, human scale. The postures of prayer have a geometry of their own, with the body arcing and bending, stretching and folding in resonance with the underlying principles of the decorated walls which surround the worshipper. Tiled walls then, become more than merely decorative; they are handmade echoes of the spiritual alchemy taking place within the soul of the worshipper, the purification and elevation of the human clay.

6.12
Domes of Shah Jahan Mosque, Thattha, Pakistan. The copper and cobalt glazes here are very similar to the glazes in the tiles from Kashan.

6.13 **Safavid Tile**

Typical of Haft Rang (seven-color) tiles that decorate the celebrated 17th-century mosques of Isfahan, this tile depicts floral decoration, including a large floral spray rising from the bottom of the field, and surrounded by further smaller sprays and single leaves all set against a rich, dappled cobalt blue ground.

Iran, 17th century
Fritware, cuerda seca (dry cord) technique
Height: 25 cm, Width: 24.7 cm
Ithra Museum 2019.0040

6.14 **Damascus Tile**
This tile would have been part of a larger panel. Its unusual design is influenced by Turkish Iznik ceramics and depicts a number of large carnation sprays, the flowers in aubergine with mid-blue and sage green calyxes. They emerge from cobalt stems with green and mid-blue leaves, bending against an unseen breeze.

Damascus, Syria, 1570–1580
Fritware painted under glaze
Height: 26 cm, Width: 26 cm
Ithra Museum 2019.0041

6.15 **Iznik Tile**
Once belonging to the family of the famous 19th-century British general Lord Kitchener, this tile was made in Iznik, which was famous for Ottoman ceramic production. It depicts large sprays of hyacinths, red lilies with cobalt calyxes, and emerald green serrated stems, which issue forth from a composite lotus flower at the bottom.

Iznik, Turkey, 17th century
Fritware painted under glaze
Height: 24 cm, Width: 24 cm
Ithra Museum 2019.0042

6.16 **Safavid Tile**

This Safavid-era tile represents the top right corner of a much larger floral panel featuring multicolored stylized leaf and floral sprays on a white background.

Iran, 17th century
Cuerda seca (dry cord) painted
Height: 20.5 cm, Width: 20.5 cm
Ithra Museum 2019.0043

6.17 **Iznik Tile**

Made in Iznik, Turkey, this tile would originally have been used as part of a larger border pattern surrounding an inner design painted on larger square tiles. Iznik tiles often took inspiration from Chinese ceramic designs, such as is seen here with the swirling, scrolling cloud band motifs.

Iznik, Turkey, c. 1580
Fritware painted under glaze
Height: 12 cm, Length: 27 cm
Ithra Museum 2019.0044

6.18 **Dome of the Rock Tiles**
These two hexagonal tiles originally date to the 16th-century restoration of the exterior walls of the Dome of the Rock in Jerusalem by the Ottoman ruler Suleiman the Magnificent.

Jerusalem, 16th century
Fritware painted under glaze
Diameter: 16 cm
Ithra Museum 2019.0049, 2019.0050

6.19 **Qur'an Verses on Tile Panel**
This panel contains verses from the Holy Qur'an enjoining man to remember God in the mosques they are decreed to build and maintain: "In the houses which Allah has ordered to be raised, in them His Name is remembered. Therein glorify Him in the mornings and in the afternoons or the evenings." (Surah An-Nur (24): 36).

Egypt, 14th century
Fritware, painted and cut tile mosaic
Length: 60 cm, Height: 10 cm
Museum of Islamic Art, Cairo 3794

6.20 **Tile Panel**

Attributed to Mamluk Egypt, and clearly inspired by Chinese blue-and-white ceramics, this rare tile panel features a range of decorative motifs including floral and plant forms and a mosque at its center.

Egypt, 14th century
Fritware painted under glaze
Height: 90 cm, Length: 120 cm
Museum of Islamic Art, Cairo 15664

6.21 **Tile Spandrel**
This Ottoman tile spandrel, depicting flowers and twisting plant tendrils, would have been placed over a doorway, window or possibly a *mihrab* niche in a mosque.

Iznik, Turkey, 17th century
Fritware painted under glaze
Height: 60 cm, Width: 50 cm
Museum of Islamic Art, Cairo 15527

6.22 **Tile Panel**

Beginning in the middle of the 16th century, the potters in Iznik began producing colored fritware tiles like these to decorate the imperial buildings designed by the chief Ottoman architect, Mimar Sinan.

Iznik, Turkey, 17th century
Fritware painted under glaze
Height: 160 cm, Width: 100 cm
Museum of Islamic Art, Cairo 15912

6.23 **Tile Panel**

Colorful, repeat patterns such as these still enliven the walls of Ottoman mosques in Istanbul, Cairo and even Medina. Although originally found in Egypt, these tiles were probably products of the Ottoman kilns in Iznik or Diyarbakir, Turkey, or possibly Damascus, Syria.

Iznik, Turkey or Damascus,
17th century
Fritware painted under glaze
Height: 160 cm, Width: 100 cm
Museum of Islamic Art, Cairo 15902

6.24 **Tile Panel**
Almost certainly decorating a Timurid-era mosque façade, these luster tiles belong to a single calligraphic frieze featuring Surat al-Kursi (the Throne verse) from the Holy Qur'an.

Kashan, Iran, late 13th or early 14th century
Fritware with colored glaze and luster
Length: 85 cm, Height: 30 cm
Museum of Islamic Art, Cairo
16296, 16297 and 16298

6.25 **Calligraphic Panel**
The Ottoman-era tile panel reads: O ‘Ibadi who have transgressed against themselves! Despair not of the Mercy of Allah: Verily, Allah forgives all sins. Truly He is Oft-Forgiving, Most Merciful (the Holy Qur'an, Surat Az-Zumar (39): 53).

Turkey or Egypt, 17th century
Fritware painted under glaze
Length: 120 cm, Height: 60 cm
Museum of Islamic Art, Cairo 16376

6.26 **Calligraphic Panel**

Probably shown on a mosque façade, this carved stone panel displays a verse from the Holy Qur'an in an ornate, florid, early Kufic style.

Egypt, Date unknown
Stone
Length: 90 cm, Height: 30 cm
Museum of Islamic Art, Cairo 14571

6.27 **Calligraphic Panel**

This carved marble panel dates from the Mamluk era in Egypt and may have been placed on the façade of a mosque. The inscription reads: "In the Name of Allah, the Most Merciful, the Most Compassionate."

Egypt, 15th century
Marble
Length: 27 cm, Height: 11 cm
Museum of Islamic Art, Cairo 2330

7 The Mosque Lamp: A Poetic Reading into its Shades and Meanings

Mohammed Abdel Bari

> Allah is the Light of the heavens and the earth. The parable of His light is as a niche and within it a lamp: the lamp is in a glass, the glass as it were a brilliant star, lit from a blessed tree, an olive, neither of the east nor of the west, whose oil would almost glow forth, though no fire touched it. Light upon light! Allah guides to His light whom He wills. And Allah sets forth parables for mankind, and Allah is All-knower of everything.
> In houses which Allah has ordered to be raised, in them His Name is remembered. Therein glorify Him in the mornings and in the afternoons or the evenings.
> (Holy Qur'an, chapter An-Nur, verses 35–6)

One might think that the sole purpose of a lamp hanging from the ceiling of the 14th-century Sultan al-Nasir Muhammad ibn Qalawun Mosque during the Mamluk era was to provide light for the worshippers, but this would do it a grave injustice. Such a view limits the lamp to its functionality without taking into consideration the aesthetic aspects of this magnificent masterpiece that used to decorate the ceiling of this prestigious ancient Cairo mosque.

Mosque lamps are pieces of art fashioned of glass and carry inside them the wick and oil, which was traditionally aromatic, needed for lighting. In Arabic, a mosque lamp is traditionally referred to by the word *mishkah*, whose meaning was originally "niche" but later expanded to include the lamps that are placed inside those niches at mosques. Their function was to protect the light inside from being blown out by the wind and to disseminate the light to a larger area. The body of the lamp was made of glass and had handles around it that allowed it to be hung from the ceiling using copper or silver chains.

← Detail of 7.1

The lamp was decorated with inscriptions comprised of either religious writings, such as verses from the Holy Qur'an, or references to historical facts which were usually related to sultans and princes. Lamps were among the traditional means used to keep the legacies of those sultans and princes alive in the collective memory.

This immortalization was done either directly by decorating the lamps with the name of the sultan in whose era they were commissioned, or indirectly by affixing a *reng* which represented families who held certain occupations. *Reng* is a Persian word meaning "color," and was used by the Mamluks to refer to the emblem that an owner would place on his houses and belongings. The most famous *rengs* were the cup for the Saqi (water bearer), the sword for Silahdar (arms bearer) and the inkwell for the Katib (writer).

The lamp

The lamp before us (opposite), which bears the name of Sultan al-Nasir Muhammad ibn Qalawun, is made of gilded polished glass and overlaid with enamel. The lamp has the shape of a vase and consists of three parts: the neck, the body and the base. The neck has a conical shape with a wide opening narrowing at the lower part to join with the body. The body has an inflated form, which narrows at its upper and lower parts to join the neck and the base. It has several handles with metal chains joined together.

The neck is decorated with a Mamluk inscription of verse 35 from Surah An-Nur, written on a background decorated with vegetal patterns. The body also has an inscription carrying the name and titles of Sultan al-Nasir Muhammad ibn Qalawun, and a similar inscription is found on the handles.

Let us look closer at the lamp and allow our eyes to wander freely in its every nook and cranny to explore the smallest of its details; the near and the far, the obvious and the hidden. A whirlpool of colored shadows overwhelm our consciousness – endless circles of spatial, temporal, cognitive and artistic connotations intertwine in our subconscious to paint a harmonious picture, filling us with feelings of serenity, gratitude, love and familiarity.

7.1 **Sultan al-Nasir Muhammad ibn Qalawun Mosque Lamp**
Written in Thulth script, the name of Sultan al-Nasir Muhammad ibn Qalawun is inscribed alongside verse 35 of Surah 24 of the Holy Qur'an: "Allah is the Light of the heavens and the earth." This mosque lamp originally hung somewhere in the Qalawun complex in Cairo.

Egypt or Syria, 1304
Glass, gilded and enameled
Height: 34 cm, Depth: 20 cm
Museum of Islamic Art, Cairo 313

Verse 35 of Surah An-Nur, reading "Allah is the Light of the heavens and the earth" and inscribed on the upper part of the lamp, takes me to the highest possible peak of enlightenment and at the same time plunges me into a pool of beautiful overlapping meanings: metaphors from the verse about the lamp, the glass, the pearly star and the blessed olive tree neither of the east nor of the west, whose oil would almost glow forth though no fire touched it.

Not only has this verse found its way to the majority of the lamps in the Muslim world due to its expressing the very idea of the lamp, but it is also the most fitting verse because of the spiritual connotations which place it at the heart of the *Irfaan* (mysticism) practice in Islamic civilization. As I look again at this engraved verse, several interpretations cross my mind, including those of Al-Junaid, Al-Qushayri, Al-Harith al-Muhasibi, Abu Madyan Al-Ghawth, Ibn 'Ajibah and other Islamic scholars who stood humbly before this particular verse. This verse is like a beautiful enigma for those with esoteric knowledge of its secrets. To convey to us the secrets of its beauty and sublimity, they might quote the renowned Cairene poet Ibn Al-Farid:

> Never will he be lost at night, for a star he is holding;
> They ask me to describe it, saying I know how to do it best,
> Indeed, I am familiar with its description;
> Pure, though not water; soft, though not wind;
> Light without fire; soul without body;
> May he shed rivers of tears, he who wasted his life,
> Without having ever experienced it.

When I see the verse written on the entire body of the lamp, I cannot help but remember Imam Al-Ghazali's book *Mishkat Al-Anwar* in which he tried to build a theory of knowledge, within the vast parameters of Islamic thought, through his detailed and exquisite interpretation of the same verse. The descriptions of the light, the lamp and the tree match the functions of understanding the material, the spiritual and the intellectual. Mosques are the natural place for the lamp, as they were also the centers of knowledge and learning in the Islamic world.

Historical background

As my eyes follow the polished glass of the lamp, I take a walk through history to Mamluk Cairo, which was at its peak of civilization and prosperity, bustling with artists, craftsmen, calligraphers and engineers who competed to demonstrate their artistic and creative talents under the patronage of sultans who appreciated architecture.

My mental journey through time would not be complete without paying tribute to the Sultan al-Nasir Mosque (Figure 7.2), which was the jewel in the crown of old Cairo. Commissioned by Sultan al-Nasir, the enormous pillars were carried from the abandoned city of priests in the region of El Ashmunein (Hermopolis) in an awe-inspiring scene as the sultan ordered engineers, quarrymen and thousands of people to carry them to the coast of the Great Sea. Big ships were prepared to carry these pillars to Cairo as soon as the season of the flooding of the Nile began, as narrated by Al-Dawadari.

As I stare at the domes, corridors and minarets of the mosque, I am reminded of Al-Qalqashandi's description of it in his book *Subh Al-Asha*: "one of the greatest, finest and most ornamented mosques. It is wide with high-rise construction and a floor furnished with high-quality marble. At the center of the ceiling, which is inlaid with gold, is a dome sitting next to an enclosure perforated with well-made iron windows. The courtyard opens to corridors from all directions."

My spatial journey would not be complete without imagining how this lamp swayed over the heads of worshippers who were washed with the light of kindness, hope and love; the scholars who sat in different circles teaching faith, jurisprudence, theology, language and logic; and the children who expressed their childish innocence and playfulness in its vast courtyard.

I stand before the al-Nasir Mosque and remember how the mosque made poets' souls soar high; starting with Hassan ibn Thabit who on visiting the Prophet's Mosque in Medina, and seeing his *minbar*, lamented the death of the Prophet Mohammed (ﷺ), saying:

> It stands so clear, the contours firm – and there
> His precinct with a prayer-place and a mosque.

Ahmad Shawqi, brimming with pride, said:

> Stand up before the world and salute Al-Azhar
> And let time hear those pearls

Last but not least comes the poet and philosopher of the Indian subcontinent Mohammed Iqbal, who stood before the Mosque of Cordoba, stricken as if with the fever of nostalgia, chanting:

> You are a shelter for art lovers, and a mecca for beauty seekers. You are built from emotions, and watered with blood from the heart. Only love can turn a stone into a heart beating with love for humanity. This love is the blood relation that connects me to you, O mosque imbued with passion, pleasure and sweet gratitude.

As I stare at al-Nasir Mosque, I remember the divine quotes of Abu Hayyan al-Tawhidi. I am almost able to break the barrier of time as I see him standing under a dome just like this mosque's dome, his soul soaring with this sublime prayer:

> God, our passion for You exalts us. Our love for You revives us. We rely on You, and no other. We stand between Your hands worshipping You. You are the shelter when times are hard, and the resort when disaster strikes. Your glory humbles valleys and mountains. For You, blame and censure can be endured. We seek Your generosity. We strive for Your light. Warm our chests with Your kindness. Give us a way to Your kingdom. Bestow Your blessings on us. Bring us closer to You. Plant Your knowledge in our souls, and make our tongues speak Your praise. (Al-Daudery, 1960, 8).

Now, as I stare at this lamp, I feel like I am allowed the rare chance of traveling through the accumulating layers of time to arrive at 14th-century Cairo. When I see the name of Sultan al-Nasir Muhammad ibn Qalawun and his titles, which are inscribed on the side of the lamp, this conjures up the image of a man whose sultanate was so great that kings and dignitaries all over the world sought to correspond with him, from the kings and princes of Europe to the kings of India, China and Abyssinia who had friendly relations with his country.

7.2 **Sultan al-Nasir Muhammad ibn Qalawun Mosque**
Mosque lamps are seen hanging from the arcades that open onto the courtyard of the Sultan al-Nasir Mosque.

As the ninth sultan of the Mamluk dynasty (b. 1285 – d. 1341), he sat on the throne for more than 40 years, ruling several countries with subjects praying for him in mosques in the Levant, Iraq, Yemen and the Maghreb after successive eras of chaos. In his book *Bada'i Al-Zuhur fi Waqa'i Al-Duhur*, Ibn Iyas said: "Egypt has never been ruled by a king greater than Al-Nasir Muhammad."

He ruled for three intermittent terms, and his era witnessed an endless series of events, happenings and turmoil. Internally, he had to deal with endless conspiracies, hostilities, chaos and struggles among factions. On top of that, he had to stand resolute against the threat of external aggressions by the Mongols and Crusaders whose greed knew no end. Above all, our sultan had to find time to reform the administrative system of the state, fight corruption, and free his people from the heavy shackles of levies and taxes, as well as reform the judiciary, state affairs, land tax and other systems.

Architectural meanings

I imagine that challenges of this magnitude would have been enough to distract the sultan from the numerous joys of life which occupied other princes and sultans who ruled successively parts of the Muslim world. His dedication to facing up to the challenges was attested by the historians who documented his life. Those same historians, however, allowed that this sultan was captivated by one pleasure that filled his heart with joy: architecture. He would commission a building for hundreds of thousands of dirhams, but then have it demolished and rebuilt to his taste if it fell short of his expectations for one reason or another. In doing so, he would spare no expense as long as he satisfied his passion for architecture. Ibn Taghri noted in his book *Al-Nujum Al-Zahirah fi Muluk Miṣr wa Al-Qahirah* that "He enjoyed beauty, acquiring only the best of everything."

No other sultan commissioned as many constructions in Egypt as he did, transforming villages into self-sustaining cities – as explained by Al-Jabarti in his book *Aja'ib Al-Athar fi Al-Tarajum wa Al-Akhbar* – and making water canals and bridges to revive the lands. For over 30 years, he remained so preoccupied with architecture that princes used it as a means to win his favor. During his reign, as explained by Ibn Taghri in his aforementioned book, Egypt witnessed a cultural and urban revival never seen during the

times of all the Mamluk sultans. As a result of the policies in his third term, Egypt entered an important stage of prosperity and economic boom.

I ponder all of that as my imagination wanders among the beautiful monuments left behind by Sultan al-Nasir, including the mosque which is decorated with magnificent minarets. Abu al-Ma'ali (the sultan's nickname) left us a collection of important monuments in Egypt and the Levant, including the Al Nasiriya school whose marvelous architectural style made it a landmark in Cairo at the time.

In addition to his khanqah named Siryaqous, which was established in the north of Cairo as a resting place for Islamic scholars, al-Nasir also built the large Ashrafi Iwan (a vaulted space that opens on one side to a courtyard),

7.3 **Complex of Sultan al-Nasir Muhammad ibn Qalawun**
A massive brass lantern hangs alongside numerous mosque lamps at the entrance to the courtyard of the school at Ibn Qalawun's complex in Cairo.

which included a dome made of ivory and ebony, and al-Nasiri Square to host luxurious horse shows. The sultan was passionate about horses, with a wide knowledge of their pedigrees and breeds. When he died, there were more than 3,000 horses in his stables, as noted by Al Maqrizi in his book *Al-Suluk fi Ma'rifat Duwal Al-Muluk*.

He also developed the coast of Alexandria, Al Ablaq Palace and the Iwan for Khaskiyyah (courtiers), and built houses within the citadel for the princes whom he married to his daughters. He ordered the restoration of the Citadel Mosque, Bab Al Qarafah (cemetery door), the seven halls overlooking a square and countless buildings and monuments.

Aesthetics and functions

Tearing my gaze away from the sultan's engraved name on the lamp, I delve into other artistic details that were used to create this masterpiece. I can almost touch the majestic yet simple Thuluth font which spreads across the body of the lamp. This energetic and flowing font brings to mind the essence of Arabic Islamic art which revolves around language that breathes life into the words, animating them in an aesthetic frame. As my eyes follow the golden and blue waves intersecting on the body of the lamp, I feel like I am watching the sun draw shining golden spokes in a blue clear sky.

This lamp symbolizes the aesthetic vision of the Arab-Islamic civilization, which focuses on marrying beauty to function. Functionwise, the lamp was the most important means of lighting in the Middle Ages, especially in Egypt and the Levant. The lamp was the canvas for a wide range of calligraphy, gilding and decoration arts for centuries.

Looking at the various aspects of this masterpiece, I remember the long history of lamps in the Arab-Islamic world and how they were given generous attention by the sultans, princes and notables who dedicated *waqfs*, or endowments, from their lands and properties, and allocated their proceeds to cover the costs of these lamps and their maintenance. It was common until recently for *waqf* documents throughout the Islamic world to include the fees spent on maintaining lamps with the required oils and materials. It was also common for craftsmen, calligraphers and decorators to dedicate all their efforts to manufacturing lamps, which shows the importance of such artifacts at the time. The daily tasks of mosque attendants included maintaining these lamps. After dawn prayer, they would lower the lamps by pulling down their chains to have them cleaned and their glass polished, then put them up again before evening prayers.

In the Arab and Islamic world today, mosques still compete to use modern and sophisticated shapes that capture the essence of traditional lamps. Several Islamic countries, especially Egypt and the Levant, still celebrate the month of Ramadan by putting up these lamps in the streets.

These lamps also crossed to the other bank of the Mediterranean as their beauty took them beyond the borders of their birthplace in the Muslim world. Europeans imported lamps from Egypt and the Levant in the early days of the Renaissance. Later on, they developed the lamp-manufacturing industry in Europe by copying and imitating oriental manufacturing techniques, as was the case in Italian cities, especially Venice, which gained fame for a period of time for making lamps that decorated the city's palaces, churches and universities.

Final thoughts

I once again stand one last time before the lamp of Sultan al-Nasir Muhammad ibn Qalawun, seeing it exactly as the first time I laid my eyes on it, with its shimmering lights touching my soul and freeing me from my narrow human condition and connecting me to the entire human existence. This is the magic behind every artifact which wakes us from our sleep and throws us into an endless whirlpool of light and sanctity in which human souls are brought together and transcend the constraints of time, space and culture.

7.4 **The *Mihrab* of the Sultan Hassan Mosque**
Dozens of lamps suspended around the beautiful *mihrab* (prayer niche) of the Sultan Hassan Mosque (built 1363) in Cairo. The lamps are 20th-century replacements of the earlier Mamluk-period lamps that are now preserved in the city's Museum of Islamic Art. (See figures 7.13 and 7.14.)

7.5 **Candlestick**
Before the widespread use of electric lights, candlesticks such as this one were traditionally placed on either side of the *mihrab* (prayer niche) at the front of the mosque to provide light during dawn and evening prayers.

Egypt or Syria, 14th century
Copper alloy inlaid with silver
Height: 21.2 cm, Diameter: 19.5 cm
Museum of Islamic Art, Cairo 15097

7.6 **Candlestick**

The production of candlesticks such as this one flourished from the 13th century, until the 16th century, particularly in Syria and Egypt. This candlestick is decorated with Thulth inscriptions and inlaid with silver medallions.

Egypt or Syria, 14th century
Copper alloy inlaid with silver
Height: 28.5 cm, Diameter: 26 cm
Museum of Islamic Art, Cairo 15066

7.7 **Candlestick**

Engraved with Thulth inscriptions of royal titles and animal motifs, this candlestick would have been presented for use in mosques and religious schools in Egypt. The Mamluk rulers of Egypt and Syria became great patrons of art and architecture. Cairo was their capital, which they ruled from 1250 to 1517.

Egypt or Syria, 14th century
Copper alloy inlaid with silver
Height: 25 cm, Diameter: 25 cm
Museum of Islamic Art, Cairo 4044

7.8 **Candlestick**
This exceptionally large Mamluk-era candlestick was designed to hold a large wax candle. These candles were often heavily scented with ambergris, aloe wood and incense and decorated with colorful paper designs. Candles and candlesticks also played an important part in Mamluk ceremonies, including 'Id and Ramadan.

Cairo, 14th century
Copper alloy inlaid with gold and silver
Height: 51 cm, Diameter: 22.5 cm
Museum of Islamic Art, Cairo 15079

7.9 **Lantern**
This monumental brass lantern bears the name of Mamluk Sultan Qansuh al-Ghuri and was probably hung in his eponymous complex, which contains his mausoleum, sabil (water distribution kiosk), library, mosque and madrasa.

Cairo, 16th century
Brass
Height: 260 cm, Diameter: 108 cm
Museum of Islamic Art, Cairo 239

7.10 **Oil Lamp**

With a simple handle, a fill hole, and a small opening for the wick, these oval-shaped pottery lamps were produced for everyday use and decorated with simple patterns. A full lamp of this type would burn for two to three hours.

Egypt, 10th–12th century
Earthenware, molded and glazed with applied handle
Length: 9 cm
Museum of Islamic Art, Cairo
42/19447, 34/19447

7.11 **Stained-Glass Window**
Originally placed in a mosque or madrasa, this colored glass window depicts a mosque flanked by two cypress trees and is surmounted with the inscription: "inform the believers" from Sura 61:13 of the Holy Qur'an.

Egypt, late 17th or early 18th century
Stucco and stained glass
Height: 131 cm, Width: 65 cm
Museum of Islamic Art, Cairo 1/386

7.12 **Ostrich Egg**

Ostrich eggs are placed atop minarets in West Africa. They were also brought back from Makkah as Hajj souvenirs. This Ottoman example, decorated with Qur'anic inscriptions, was originally suspended above a mosque lamp to prevent rodents from consuming the oil placed inside.

Egypt, 19th century
Ostrich egg and paint
Length: 17 cm, Width: 13 cm
Museum of Islamic Art, Cairo 1/393

7.13 **Sultan Hassan Mosque Lamp**
This lamp owes its excellent state of preservation to the care given to it by light keepers in the Sultan Hassan Mosque, where it originally hung. Mosque endowment records often stipulate the number of lamps to be provided and when they should be lit and cleaned.

Egypt or Syria, 14th century
Enameled glass
Height: 32 cm, Diameter: 25 cm
Museum of Islamic Art, Cairo 301

7.14 **Mosque Lamp**
In addition to Surah An-Nur, or Light Verse, from the Holy Qur'an, this mosque lamp is inscribed with the name of the Mamluk Sultan Hassan, suggesting that it may have originally hung in the Sultan Hassan Mosque in Cairo.

Egypt or Syria, 14th century
Enameled glass
Height: 32 cm, Diameter: 21 cm
Museum of Islamic Art, Cairo 320

7.15 **Incense Burner**
Designed to be suspended in order to allow the aromatic smoke to diffuse widely, this incense burner was used in mosques, madrasas and residences for a variety of occasions. Different incense fragrances were used, for example sandalwood, frankincense, musk and camphor.

Egypt, 19th century
Glazed ceramic
Height: 16.5 cm, Depth: 7.5 cm
Museum of Islamic Art, Cairo 15872

7.16 **Incense Burner**
Incense was widely used in mosques across the Islamic world. Occasionally, mosque *waqfiyyas* (endowment deeds) would designate staff to burn incense regularly in important locations around the mosque.

Egypt, 14th century
Brass inlaid with silver
Diameter: 9.5 cm, Height: 18.5 cm
Museum of Islamic Art, Cairo 15291

7.17 **Incense Container**

Used to store incense, this Chinese Qing-dynasty container contains an inscription that reads: “O Allah, I ask for Heaven and what gets me closer to it through speech or action, and I seek refuge in You from the fire and what gets me closer to it through speech or action.”

China, 19th century
Copper alloy inlaid with silver
Height: 6 cm, Diameter: 10 cm
Museum of Islamic Art, Cairo 3863

7.18 **Incense Container**
Despite a stamp found on its base attributing this object to the reign of the Xuande emperor of the Ming dynasty – Zhu Zhanji (d. 1435), this piece probably dates to the 19th-century Qing era in China. The black inscription spanning the bowl holds the *shahada*, the Islamic declaration of faith. "There is no God but Allah and Mohammed is His Messenger."

China, 19th century
Enameled cloisonné
Height: 7 cm, Diameter: 15.5 cm
Museum of Islamic Art, Cairo 3456

8 The *Mihrab*: Reflections on Form, Function and Symbolism

Oludamini Ogunnaike

This beautiful wooden *mihrab* is from the Mosque of Sayyida Ruqayya bint 'Ali ibn Abi Ṭalib in Cairo. As indicated by the floriated Kufic calligraphy on a frieze on the front of the *mihrab*, it was commissioned by Sayyida 'Ulam al-Amiriyya (d. 1140), the wife of the Fatimid Caliph Abu 'Ali Mansur al-Amir bi'Ahkam Allah (d. 1130), but was not completed until the reign of the Caliph al-Fa'iz (1154–60) and his vizier al-Salih Ṭala'i'.

Nearly five centuries separate the construction of this *mihrab* and the death of the one in whose mosque and mausoleum it was placed, and it was made nearly a millennium before this exhibition. Yet this *mihrab* does not just take us back in time to the days of the Fatimid Caliphate: it has a beauty that is, to a certain degree, timeless. The curling arabesques, the interlacing geometric patterns and the striking Kufic calligraphy, while all characteristic of this particular time period and regional style, reflect something more transcendent, which is one of the reasons why the intricate beauty of this *mihrab* has captivated lovers of art and worshippers across the centuries.

This *mihrab* is of particular interest to me, as a Harvard-trained scholar of the Islamic intellectual and artistic traditions of North and West Africa, due to the harmonious way it combines the three main features of Islamic artistic design: calligraphy, arabesque, and geometric design. It includes an early example of geometric tessellation on a curved wooden surface, which requires a working knowledge of non-Euclidean geometry (which only began to be formulated in Europe in the 19th century [Rosenfield. 1996, 447–94]). I remember the first time I saw such a pattern in person, on a field trip to the New York Metropolitan Museum of Art in middle school. The patterns literally stopped me in my tracks. It was as if I was seeing the world of mathematics made tangible for the first time. That pattern, like the tessellated geometric designs on this *mihrab*, and like the thousands of other geometric patterns so characteristic of the flourishing of Islamic art

← Detail of 8.1

after the 10th century, allowed me to pick out multiple distinct patterns depending on the perspective I took. The indefinite tessellations meant that the center could be almost anywhere, and depending on how my eye grouped the lines and shapes, different patterns would emerge. At the time, I just thought of it as a neat visual trick, but after my studies of Islamic art and philosophy, this feature strikes me as being profoundly symbolic of a worldview inspired by the Holy Qur'an in which everything is connected ("Who created seven heavens one upon another. You do not see in the creation of the All-merciful any imperfection. Then look again; do you see any gaps?" [67:3]), everything is apportioned ("Verily, we have created everything according to a measure" [54:49]), and in which everything can be seen from multiple distinct, yet non-contradictory perspectives ("To God belong the East and the West. Wheresoever you turn, there is the Face of God" [2:115] "And among His signs are the creation of the heavens and the earth and the variation in your tongues and colors. Truly in that are signs for those who know" [30:22]).

The history of the *mihrab*

8.1 **Portable *Mihrab***
This prayer niche bears an inscription in Kufic script explaining that it was commissioned by al-Amiriyya, wife of the Fatamid Caliph al-Amir bi-Ahkam Allah. Intended for the Mosque of al-Sayyida Ruqayya, this *mihrab* was likely used on occasions such as 'Id, when it could be put outside for the crowds that could not fit inside the mosque. (For the reverse side of the *mihrab*, see Figure 8.5.)

Cairo, 1154
Carved, painted and joined wood
Height: 210 cm, Width: 111 cm, Length: 54 cm
Museum of Islamic Art, Cairo 446

To better understand this work of art, we should first place it in the historical context of the development of the *mihrab*. The etymology of the word *mihrab* has been debated by linguists for centuries, with some favoring the creative interpretation of the word coming from the root *h-r-b* (to wage war), interpreting the *mihrab* as a place or instrument for waging the "greater holy war" against the *nafs* (ego, carnal self). However, the appearances of this word in pre-Islamic poetry and the Holy Qur'an (3:37, 3:39, 19:11, 34:13, 38:21) seem to indicate that it meant a "sanctuary," like a throne room or the Holy of Holies in Jerusalem (the Holy Qur'an uses the word *mihrab* to describe the sanctuary of the temple of Jerusalem in which Zakariya and Maryam worshipped [3:37, 3:39, 19:11]) and the derivative sanctuaries in Eastern churches. Modern linguists argue that the word *mihrab* is derived from the Old Ethiopic *mehram*, which means a "holy place or sanctuary" (not unlike the Arabic *haram*), the transposition of the "m" with the "b" being common in Southern Arabian dialects (e.g. "Bakka" [3:96] and "Makkah") (Khoury. 1998, 5–6).

According to some of the earliest sources, the first Islamic *mihrab* may have been a simple stone slab or sign put on the qibla wall of the Prophet's (ﷺ) Mosque to indicate the direction of prayer (towards the Ka'ba in Makkah)

(Khoury. 1998, 4). In some narrations, it was a spear, which gives another explanation for the etymology of *mihrab*, a spear being an instrument of war. The characteristic concave niche shape of the *mihrab* is attributed to the renovation of the Prophet's (ﷺ) Mosque during the reign of the Caliph al-Walid (d. 715), when the governor of Medina, 'Umar ibn 'abd al-'Aziz (d. 720), ordered a niche to be constructed in the qibla wall. Many early *mihrabs*, such as that in the cave underneath the Dome of the Rock (*Qubbat as-Sakhrah*) in Jerusalem, were constructed as false doors or archways carved in relief on the qibla wall of the mosque. The niche form has several pre-Islamic antecedents: the ark of synagogues, the apse of churches, the throne niche of palaces, the niches holdings statues in Greco-Roman temples, the *iwans* of Sassanid architecture, the exedra of Roman basilicas, etc., but also has strong resonances with the Holy

8.2 **Mount Hira, Saudi Arabia**
This photograph taken in 1970 shows Mount Hira, where the Prophet (ﷺ) received the first Qur'anic revelation in a cave at its summit. The concave form of the *mihrab* serves as a reiteration of the cave as verses of the Holy Qur'an continue to reverberate in mosques around the world.

Qur'anic "niche" (*mishkat*) of the celebrated verse of light, "God is the Light of the heavens and the earth. The parable of His Light is a niche, wherein is a lamp ..." (24:35), which adorns many *mihrabs*. This resonance is enhanced by common practice of placing or hanging lamps within the *mihrab*. Holy Qur'anic verses that explicitly mention the *mihrab*, such as "Whenever Zachariah went in to her in the Sanctuary (*mihrab*), he found her provisioned" (3:37), "And the angels called to him, standing in the Sanctuary at worship" (3:39), and "So he came forth unto his people from the Sanctuary, then he made signal to them, 'Give you glory at dawn and evening'" (19:11), also commonly feature on *mihrabs*.

As the place where the imam stands in leading congregational prayer, reciting the Holy Qur'an, the *mihrab* is associated with the place of the revelation of the Holy Qur'an, whose first verses Muslims believe were revealed to the Prophet Mohammed (ﷺ) in the cave of Hira just outside of Makkah (Figure 8.2). Thus, in addition to marking the direction of prayer, the *mihrab*'s concave form functions as a kind of "reiteration" of the cave of the first revelation, in which the verses of the Holy Qur'an continue to reverberate. Many early *mihrabs*, such as the fixed stucco *mihrab* of the Mausoleum of Sayyida Ruqayya (the same structure to which this portable *mihrab* belongs), are adorned with a canopy in the form of a seashell. While this motif was common in Hellenistic art, in the Islamic context it takes on the added symbolism of the shell enclosing the pearl, which is a Holy Qur'anic symbol of Paradise (52:24, 56:23, 76:19), and as Burckhardt writes,

> Is one of the Islamic symbols of the Divine Word; according to a saying of the Prophet (ﷺ), the world was created from a white pearl. The seashell enclosing the pearl is like the "ear" of the heart receiving the Divine Utterance; it is, in fact, in the *mihrab* that this utterance is made. (Burckhardt. 2009, 94)

Moreover, just as the "sound of the sea" can be heard in the shell, the sound of the Divine Revelation echoes through the *mihrab*.

Many *mihrabs* contain two columns on either side of the niche, topped by a semicircular horseshoe or pointed keel arch, and these features recall the arched doorways and arcades (*riwaq*) of columns so characteristic of Islamic architecture. The Umayyads quickly adopted Byzantine vegetal mosaics, and similar stylized vines and plant motifs appear in the arabesques of early monuments of the Dome of the Rock, and the *mihrabs*

of the Great Mosques of Kairouan and Cordoba (Figure 8.3). Recalling the Holy Qur'anic symbols of Paradise (2:266) and the "good word" of the revelation itself (14:24), these arabesques reinforce the connection between the *mihrab* as the place of recitation of the Holy Qur'an, and its role as a sanctuary, a kind of prefiguration of the paradisal state. As the art of geometric patterns developed in sophistication, these patterns also adorned *mihrabs* – in stone, tile, stucco and wood. This beautiful wooden *mihrab* is portable (presumably for use on feast days when it could be put outside for the crowds that could not fit inside the mosque), like the earliest *mihrabs*, but is also adorned with the complex and sophisticated mix of geometric design, arabesques and calligraphy that came to characterize later *mihrabs*.

Historical context of the mausoleum of Sayyida Ruqayya

This *mihrab* is one of the peaks of the art of the Fatimid Caliphate, the great patrons of Islamic arts who ruled North Africa from 909 to 1171, expanding from the Maghreb to Egypt and the Middle East. Fatimid art took up elements and techniques from Umayyad, Abbasid, Byzantine, Coptic and North African art forms and developed a creative and innovative synthesis that would heavily influence the later Islamic art of later North African dynasties, especially the Mamluk dynasty (and through them the art of the Ottoman Empire). As the founders of Cairo, which they made their capital in 969, the Fatimids left an indelible stamp on the city through their art, architecture and urban planning. The unique artistic "brand" of the Fatimids included a distinctive kind of Kufic script, known as Fatimid Kufic, which was commonly employed on monuments, buildings, and on this *mihrab*. The Fatimids also took great care to construct beautiful mausolea (*mashhads*) for members of the family of the Prophet (ﷺ) (*Ahl al-Bayt*) in Cairo, such as the mausolea of Sayyida Ruqayya (from which this *mihrab* comes), the daughter of 'Ali ibn Abi Ṭalib, the Prophet's son-in-law and cousin, and the fourth and last of the four "rightly guided caliphs" of the Muslim community. Sayyida Ruqayya is believed to have come to Cairo along with her stepsister Zaynab after the tragic events of the Battle of Karbala. Sayyida Ruqayya, her step-brother Husayn ibn 'Ali (d. 680), her stepsister, Zaynab bint 'Ali (d. 682), and her grand-niece Sayyida Nafisa (d. 824) are regarded as "patron saints" of the city, and are widely venerated to this day, with Cairenes regularly visiting their mausolea.

8.3 **The *Mihrab* within the Great Mosque of Cordoba**
With its rich mosaic decoration, carved stucco, sculpted marble and calligraphy, the *mihrab* of the Great Mosque of Cordoba is a spectacular artistic masterpiece.

An inscription painted under the ribs of the dome of the mausoleum of Sayyida Ruqayya indicates that it was constructed in 1133 (Williams. 1985, 44) but another inscription on a cenotaph inside the mausoleum gives a later date of commission (1138–9) and tells us more about the context of its construction:

> This is the tomb of Sayyida Ruqayya, daughter of the Commander of the Believers, ʻAli ibn Abi Talib, God's blessings be upon him and … and God bless our Lord Mohammed (ﷺ), Seal of the Prophets [33:33] "O People of the House, God only desires to put away from you abomination and with cleansing to cleanse you." [44:51–4] "Surely the God-fearing shall be in a station secure among gardens and fountains, robed in silk and brocade, set face to face. Even so; and we shall espouse them to wide-eyed houris." [Side 3, 113:1–3] "Say: 'I take refuge with the Lord of the Daybreak from the evil of what He has created, from the evil of darkness when it gathers, from the evil

8.4 **Dome of al-Sayyida Ruqayya**
Built in 1133 during the Fatimid period by order of al-Hafiz li-Din Allah, Cairo's Mosque of al-Sayyida Ruqayya originally housed the portable *mihrab* discussed in this chapter.

> of women who blow on knots.'" The building of this blessed tomb was ordered by the noble [female] personage, the Amiriyya, whose agent was the Qadi Maknun, servant of al-Hafiz, by the hand of the excellent Abu Turab Haydara ibn Abi'l-Fath; may God have mercy upon him, in the year 533 [1138–9]. [11:73] "The mercy of God and His blessings be upon you, O People of the House!" [7:54] "Surely your Lord is God, who created the heavens and the earth in six days – Then sat Himself upon the Throne, covering the day with the night it pursues urgently- and the sun, and the moon, and the stars." (Williams. 1985, 47)

The Mamluk historian al-Maqrizi (d. 1442) describes the patron of this mausoleum, the widow of al-Amir, as "a woman of piety, generosity, virtue, and full of the fear of God. She used to send to members of the Prophet's family for prayers." (Williams. 1985, 47).

Features of this *mihrab*

Geometric design

One of the most striking features of this *mihrab* is the beautifully engraved sixfold "star-patterns" on the back and sides of the structure. Such designs would become quite prominent in later Mamluk, Ayyubid and Ottoman woodwork. The front surface of the *mihrab* also features a lovely and ingenious tessellation of regular polygons, structured with sixfold symmetry (the design looks the same if rotated 60 degrees). The curved interior surface of the *mihrab* features a simpler sixfold pattern, which, as mentioned above, is an early example of non-Euclidean geometric tessellation.

In addition to being the basis for most geometric tessellations, the ubiquitous sixfold geometric patterns have been taken to symbolize the six days of creation cited in the Holy Qur'anic verse on the middle band of the front of this *mihrab* ("Truly your Lord is God, Who created the heavens and the earth in six days, then mounted the Throne. He causes the night to cover the day, which pursues it swiftly; and the sun, the moon, and the stars are made subservient by His Command. Do not creation and command belong to Him? Blessed is God, Lord of the worlds!" [7:54]), as well as the six cardinal directions (north, south, east, west, zenith, nadir). The Ikhwan al-Safa' and Ibn al-'Arabi also relate these six cardinal directions to the seven days of the week and the seven Divine Attributes: Life, Seeing, Will,

Power, Knowledge, Speech and Hearing, with the most central attribute, Life, being located at the central point where all the directions converge. From this symbolic perspective, it is significant that the sixfold geometric patterns of this *mihrab* are filled with plants, a symbol of life. In this way, these patterns can be seen as representing the seven Divine Attributes.

The number six is also the first perfect number (the sum of its factors is equal to itself), and in the science of letters (*'ilm al-huruf*) that was highly developed under the Fatimids, and later taken up by figures such as Ibn al-'Arabi and Ahmad al-Buni, the number six corresponds to the letter *waw*, and was taken as a symbol of the Perfect Human (*al-Insan al-Kamil*), given that *waw* serves to connect words and sentences in Arabic just as the Perfect Human connects heaven and earth in this Islamic cosmology. Moreover, *waw* is the last letter in the ordering of the 28 Arabic letters based on their place of articulation, from innermost to outermost, just as humankind is the last of God's creation to appear, and the Prophet Mohammed (ﷺ), the Perfect Human *par excellence*, is the last of the Prophets.

Moreover, many sixfold geometric tessellations, such as those adorning this *mihrab*, feature pentagons and hexagons. In the science of letters, the number five corresponds to the letter *ha'*, which is the first of the letters in the ordering mentioned above, as it comes from the deepest point of articulation, in the chest. When combined with the *waw* of the six, this spells the Arabic word *Huwa*, the third person pronoun, which combines the first and the last, and is considered by many commentators on the Holy Qur'an to be a name for the Divine Essence (Akkach. 2005, 147). It is thus fitting that the *mihrab*, which marks the place of encounter with the Divine, has this particular geometric-numerical-alphabetical symbolism. While the craftsmen who made this *mihrab* may not have had these symbolic notions in mind, given the prevalence of such notions in the influential writings of Islamic thinkers and philosophers from the 10th century down to the present day, it is likely that many visitors to this *mihrab* would interpret its patterns according to this or a similar schema.

The interlocking designs on the top and bottom friezes on the back of the *mihrab* create simpler tessellations of a single shape, whose negative space becomes the positive space of its inverted neighbor (as in the yin-yang symbol or the patterns of M. C. Escher), which can be interpreted as an illustration of the Holy Qur'anic declaration that *"of all things We*

8.5 **The Reverse Side of the Portable *Mihrab***
Unlike other *mihrabs* which are permanent features within the front wall of the mosque, this portable *mihrab* is freestanding and designed to be seen from both sides. As such, the reverse side displays a diverse range of geometric designs, arabesques and calligraphy that came to characterize later *mihrabs*. (For the front side of the *mihrab*, see Figure 8.1.)

created pairs" (51:49). This complementary duality is also represented in the relationship between these geometric designs and the intricate arabesques that fill them.

Arabesques

One of the great artistic developments represented in the woodwork of this *mihrab* is the integration of the intricately spiraling arabesques within these geometric patterns. These arabesques are a kind of archetypal geometrization of the vegetal form, as Burckhardt writes:

> In its more stylized versions, an arabesque in plant forms bears no more than a distant likeness to a plant. But it does represent a perfect transcription of the laws of rhythm into visual terms. Its unfolding is continuous, like a wave, with contrasting phases having various degrees of resonance. The design does not need to be symmetrical, but, to make up for this, it always has certain repetitions ... (Burckhardt. 2009, 66)

As Burckhardt has also argued, the curving arabesque is more feminine or *Jamali* than the more "masculine" or *Jalali* rigor of the straight lines of the geometric designs. The filling of these geometric patterns with the spiraling vines of the arabesques can be likened to the protective shell and the sweet fruit or kernel, or the tendency in much of traditional Islamic domestic architecture for an austere exterior to open up onto a vibrant interior of color, plant-life and fountains. This relationship is also paralleled in the Hadith which declare God to be intrinsically beautiful and merciful, and extrinsically majestic and severe, "Verily God is Beautiful, and he loves Beauty" and "My Mercy precedes my wrath." However, as many Islamic scholars have argued, even God's wrath is a form of Divine Mercy, which as the Holy Qur'an says, "encompasses all things" (7:156). The fact that the arabesque is a stylized representation of the very substance of the *mihrab* (wood, a tree) is also relevant here; if the arabesque can symbolize Divine Life and Mercy, then the wooden substance of the *mihrab* can serve as a representation of Islamic cosmologies in which the cosmos itself and all life therein is derived from this Divine Life and Mercy.

8.6 ***Mihrab***
This Ilkhanid-era prayer niche, or *mihrab*, is signed by its maker, Ibn Abu Nasr, and includes inscriptions taken from Surat al-Ma'idah (5:55) relating the importance of prayer and zakat, or charitable tithing, which are two of the five pillars of Islam. Surat al-Jumu'a (62:9) is also featured enjoining Muslims to attend the Friday sermon and prayer.

Iran, 1319
Underglaze painted
Height: 100 cm, Width: 63 cm
Museum of Islamic Art, Cairo 3754

Calligraphy

Another striking feature of this *mihrab* is the calligraphy in the Kufic style that characterized Fatimid monuments. To put it poetically, this style of calligraphy is like the child produced by the marriage of the geometric patterns and arabesques. While this style of floriated Kufic, like other forms of Kufic calligraphy, brings out the geometric regularity of the Arabic script (square Kufic being the extreme example of this feature), the untrained eye may have difficulty separating the calligraphic inscriptions from the surrounding arabesques, so well are the two features blended on this *mihrab*. As Burckhardt writes, "The bringing together of writing and stylized vegetation evokes the analogy which exists between the 'book of the world' and the 'world-tree,' two symbols well known to Muslim esotericism" (Burckhardt. 2009, 57). This connection between the symbols of the "book of the world" and the "world-tree" can be seen in the following verses of the Holy Qur'an: "Hast thou not considered how God sets forth a parable? A good word is as a good tree: its roots firm and its branches in the sky" (14:24) and "We shall show them Our signs upon the horizons and within themselves till it becomes clear to them that it is the truth. Does it not suffice that thy Lord is Witness over all things?" (41:53).

As for the text of the calligraphy, the central panel just above the *mihrab*'s arch reads:

> One of the things commissioned by the honourable, protected, and great personage, al-Amiriyya, whose service was undertaken by al-Qadi Abu'l-Hasan Maknun and who is served now, by the correct commander, the righteous of the realm, Abu'l-Hasan, the right hand of al-Fa'iz, al-Ṣalih, intended for the *mashhad* of al-Sayyida Ruqayya, the daughter of the Commander of the Faithful, 'Ali. (Hammad. 2019)

The outermost frame of calligraphy contains the celebrated "Throne Verse" (*Ayat Al-Kursi*) and the following two verses, which read:

> God, there is no God but He, the Living, the Self-Subsisting. Neither slumber overtakes Him nor sleep. Unto Him belongs whatsoever is in the heavens and whatsoever is on the earth. Who is there who may intercede with Him save by His leave? He knows that which is before them and that which is behind them. And they encompass nothing of His Knowledge, save what He wills. His Pedestal embraces the heavens and the earth. Protecting them tires Him not, and He is the Exalted, the Magnificent. There is no coercion in religion. Sound judgment has become clear from error. So whosoever disavows false deities and believes in God has grasped the most unfailing handhold, which never breaks. And God is Hearing, Knowing. God is the Protector of those

8.7 ***Mihrab* Panel**
This marble panel may have originally been placed on the qibla wall of a mosque. The inscription in the form of a mosque lamp is a mirror image of the *shahada*: "There is no God but Allah." It is also adorned with a verse from the Holy Qur'an (3:37) that mentions the *mihrab*.

Cairo, 16th century
Carved marble
Length: 66 cm, Height: 57 cm
Museum of Islamic Art, Cairo 4330

> who believe. He brings them out of the darkness into the light. As for those who disbelieve, their protectors are the idols, bringing them out of the light into the darkness. They are the inhabitants of the Fire, abiding therein. (2:255–7)

These verses were quite common on Fatimid *mihrabs*, mosques and monuments. Continuing the theme of Divine Sovereignty, light, and exhortations to piety, the middle band of calligraphy reads:

> Truly your Lord is God, Who created the heavens and the earth in six days, then mounted the Throne. He causes the night to cover the day, which pursues it swiftly; and the sun, the moon, and the stars are made subservient by His Command. Do not creation and command belong to Him? Blessed is God, Lord of the worlds! Call upon your Lord humbly and in secret. Truly He loves not the transgressors. And

> work not corruption upon the earth after it has been set aright, but call upon Him in fear and in hope. Surely the Mercy of God is ever nigh unto the virtuous (7:54–6)

These verses also commonly adorned Fatimid monuments, and also appear on the cenotaph of the shrine of Sayyida Ruqayya (Williams. 1985, 47). The innermost band of calligraphy continues the theme of light and exhortations to piety with the verses that immediately follow the celebrated "Light Verse" (*Ayat Al-Nur*), while calling attention to the function of the *mihrab*:

> [It is] in houses that God has permitted to be raised and wherein His Name is remembered. He is therein glorified, morning and evening, by men whom neither trade nor buying and selling distract from the remembrance of God, the performance of prayer, and the giving of alms, fearing a day when eyes and hearts will be turned about, that God may reward them for the best of that which they have done, and increase them from His Bounty. And God provides for whomsoever He will without reckoning. (24:36–8) God Almighty has spoken the truth and His noble messenger has conveyed it.

As mentioned above, the multilayered structure of this *mihrab* is reminiscent of that described in the "Light Verse":

> God is the Light of the heavens and the earth. The parable of His Light is a niche, wherein is a lamp. The lamp is in a glass. The glass is as a shining star kindled from a blessed olive tree, neither of the East nor of the West. Its oil would well-nigh shine forth, even if no fire had touched it. Light upon light. God guides unto His Light whomsoever He will, and God sets forth parables for mankind, and God is Knower of all things. (24:35)

The "niche," "star" and "olive tree" can be seen in the niche, geometric patterns and wooden arabesques of this *mihrab*. It is this remarkably multifaceted harmony of meaning, form and function, of calligraphy, geometry and arabesque, of creativity and craftsmanship that make this *mihrab* a masterpiece. It is not only a masterpiece of Fatimid art, nor even of Islamic art, but of human aesthetic achievement.

8.8 ***Mihrab* Plaque**
This plaque was found in the Madrasa Bedeiriyya near Cairo's Qalawun Mosque complex. It depicts a *mihrab* niche containing a mosque lamp with the inscription "God is the Light of the heavens and the earth." The lamp is flanked by two candlesticks.

Cairo, 1357
Carved marble
Height: 60 cm, Width: 35 cm
Museum of Islamic Art, Cairo 19

9 The Prayer Rug: A Microcosm of the Mosque

Mohamed Ahmed Abd el-Salam

Fix your eyes on the prayer rug before you (opposite and Figure 9.3). Now imagine entering Edirne's Selimiye Mosque half a millennium ago. You walk through the huge stone-built main entrance, and immediately see bright Ottoman tile decorations in floral and geometric shapes in the classical Islamic artistic style. Proceeding, you come to the prayer area, surrounded by beautiful columns covered in decorated wood in multiple colors. Looking up, the ceiling has a huge dome, as well as half-domes and quarter-domes. You continue in humility and awe to perform ablution and then move into the prayer area.

There are beautiful lanterns all around, as well as the large main mosque lamp which hangs in the middle of the huge dome covering the largest section of the prayer area. There are also wooden ornaments and vaultings in the corners of the prayer area. You prepare to pray two *raka'at* to greet the mosque. Under your feet are the warm fibers of this row carpet. You sense the perfume and rose water sprinkled on the carpet and in the mosque corners. This carpet is a veritable masterpiece which depicts the shape of niches, lanterns and Islamic ornaments. It is as if it holds the entire mosque just in the small area where one kneels and prays.

As someone who specializes in the study of Islamic textiles, I have had the immense privilege to examine some of the greatest examples of Islamic row carpets firsthand in collections around the world, including the Museum of Islamic Art in Cairo, the Louvre in Paris, the Victoria and Albert Museum in London and the Islamic Art Museum in Berlin. I believe that row carpets, and this masterpiece in particular, are among the greatest examples of artistic creativity from the Islamic world. Such carpets are marvels of craftsmanship, inspiration and design and are perfectly suited to their function. Each row carpet is a complete work of art, beautifully combining functional and aesthetic elements. The artist's creativity is evident in his ability to tirelessly repeat the same decorations, creating a piece of stunning creative harmony.

← Detail of 9.3

Following spread:
9.1 **The Expansive Dome of the Selimiye Mosque in Edirne, Turkey**
Considered the masterwork of the architect Mimar Sinan (d. 1588), the Selimiye Mosque was the center of the Ottoman Empire at the time of its construction in 1569.

Historical perspectives

During the time of the Prophet (ﷺ) and the Rashidun Caliphs, mosque furniture was simple and eschewed ornament. The Prophet's Mosque did not originally have carpets or rugs, and the ground was covered with sand and small pebbles. The oldest remaining parts of knotted woolen carpets, which were used to cover mosque floors, date back to the Seljuk period. They include eight carpets found in the Alaeddin Mosque in Konya, Turkey, which was built in 1219. They are now preserved in the Museum of Turkish and Islamic Art in Istanbul.

It has been documented that hand-knotted woolen carpets were present from the early centuries of Islam and were used for variety of purposes, such as covering the ground or as curtains to decorate the walls. However, row carpets as we know them today were a later development. They began with single niche prayer carpets used in mosques, palaces and homes. Afterwards, they evolved into multi-row carpets with several niches to accommodate numerous people according to the number of niches, and were decorated with aligned niches, ranging from two to ten niches or more. The number of niches was often related to the available space in the mosque, and carpets could include shapes of niches placed vertically on top of each other. Thus, a single multi-row carpet would contain multiple individual prayer rugs each with their own single niches. The earliest known collection of multiple-row niche carpets dates back to the 15th century and contains three carpets held at the Museum of Turkish and Islamic Art in Istanbul. The same period saw the establishment of specialized workshops that produced prayer rugs and row carpets. As a result, row carpets reached their artistic pinnacle in the 16th and 17th centuries. Many of the best row carpets of this period can be attributed to the Ottoman workshops of Turkey, the ateliers of Safavid Persia and Mughal India, as well as the carpets produced in Islamic Turkestan.

From China to Andalusia, mosques have a long history of being furnished with prayer rugs with either single *mihrab* niche or congregational prayer carpets, also called row carpets, with a niche for each worshipper. They can both be called *sejjadah* or *misjadah* because they refer to the place of prostration.

Ushak row carpet

This is a section of an Ushak row, or *saf*, carpet from the 16th century. It is very rare, being one of the earliest productions from the city of Usak, Turkey. Usak (written as "Uşak" in modern Turkish and pronounced "Ushak") benefited from its excellent geographical location at the crossroads between Central Anatolia and the Aegean. Being part of the Anatolian Plateau, the area has many natural pastures, as well as good climate and air quality: factors required to produce the finest carpets. Thanks to Usak's proximity to the port of Izmir, the region became famous for carpet manufacturing and exporting, especially to Europe. Indeed, prayer rugs and row carpets made in Usak inspired European painters during the Renaissance. Examples of Islamic carpets were present in the paintings of Giovanni Bellini, Vittore Carpaccio, Lorenzo Lotto and others. Moreover, individual prayer rugs and row carpets feature heavily in works by Orientalist photographers who visited the Islamic world in the 19th and 20th centuries.

9.2 **A Quiet Moment in the Selimiye Mosque**
Surrounded by colorful Iznik tiles, and cast in brilliant light streaming from a window, a man reads from the Holy Qur'an in a corner of the Selimiye Mosque. The row carpet discussed in this chapter (see Figure 9.3) originally furnished the Selimiye Mosque.

As far as we know, this masterpiece is one of four surviving fragments originally placed in the Selimiye Mosque in Edirne, Turkey, which was built in 1569–75 during the reign of Sultan Selim II (1524–74). Sinan Agha (1490–1588), the most important architect of the Ottoman era, supervised the construction. This carpet was laid in the Selimiye Mosque for worshippers to stand on in rows during congregational prayers and was thus part of a much larger multiple-niche row carpet. Parts of this carpet remained in the mosque until 1914, and four parts were later distributed to museums and art collections around the world, including the Arab World Institute in Paris, the Museum of Turkish and Islamic Art in Istanbul and the Campana Museum in Milan, Italy. The fourth fragment, shown here, belongs to Ithra's collection.

This rectangular textile is decorated with a niche in the shape of a horseshoe delineated with a zigzag line, and a triple-chain pendant lamp, similar to the actual lamps found hanging from archways inside mosques. The niche is decorated with abstract floral motifs, composed of intertwined geometric and plant forms in a brown on a dark blue/purple background, the latter taken from the natural dye extracted from the indigo plant. At its center, immediately below the niche, is an almond-shaped motif called a bukharia (bukhari ornament) which is framed with brown leaves. The space inside the bukharia is filled with green branches bearing white tulips with accents of red and brown from natural dyes extracted from rose madder, blackberries and cochineal. It also has red clove flowers on a light turquoise blue background. Both the top and bottom of the shape end with an open flower colored in red, white and turquoise. The background space inside the niche and surrounding the bukharia is decorated with open heart shaped red Allegheny monkeyflowers and white leaves on a dark blue background, a distinctive feature of Ushak carpets. The leaves on both sides are symmetrically aligned with a natural appearance. The area around the niche arch is decorated with floral motifs: two plant tendrils bear multi-petal rosettes and flowers in green, red and turquoise on a dark brown background, with both branches leaning inwards to meet at the top. Here, the background color is yellow.

There are two frames at the top of this part of the row carpet, the first is composed of two thin strips enclosing a branch bearing small Allegheny monkeyflowers and dog rose flowers – the artist highlights the flow and grace of the floral decorations, as if they are carried and caressed gently by the breeze. This is followed by a second, wider, frame – which is the outer

9.3 **Ushak Row Carpet**
This carpet fragment originally formed part of the central upper tier of a communal multiple-niche prayer rug in the Selimiye Mosque in Edirne, Turkey. The design of the rug, including its flowers, niche and lamp, would have reflected the splendor of that mosque's interior.

Oushak, Turkey, c. 1560
Wool pile
Height: 145 cm, Width: 74 cm
Ithra Museum 2019.0038

frame of this part of the carpet and also serves as the middle frame of the full row carpet. The original complete carpet would have been decorated with three frames, the largest of which being the middle frame. This part of the frame is decorated with three palm-shaped motifs surrounded by sharp spear-shaped leaves, clove flowers, tulip flowers, Allegheny monkeyflowers and bistort flowers, on elegant flowing branches.

Interestingly, decorations around the niche arch in this carpet are similar to those found in the actual niche arches of the Selimiye Mosque, and the niche arch found on one of the entrances to the mosque. Likewise, the inner windows that decorate the central dome of the mosque – which are connected by semicircular arches and topped with a decorative multi-arch shape – also echo the niche shapes seen in row carpets. This design alignment between the architecture and the row carpets confirms the unity of the overall aesthetic between the Selimiye Mosque and the specially commissioned furniture, as well as the strong bond between faith and art.

9.4 **The Exterior of the Selimiye Mosque in Edirne, Turkey**
Surrounded by four tall minarets, the Mosque of Selim II is surmounted with one of the largest domes ever built. Attached to the mosque were libraries, schools, hospices, baths, and soup kitchens for the poor, as well as markets, hospitals and a cemetery.

Methods and materials

Several materials were used in manufacturing and decorating Islamic row carpets, including wool, cotton, silk and linen. Different types of threads were also used to create the overall shape or the knots. Wool was used for the main threads on the loom, and the bulk of the surface pile was made by tightening the knots. Most of the pile came from woolen yarns, as it is the only raw material that allows the creation of the knot and pile in row carpets. Sheep's wool gives an especially soft surface, taking into account the friction and contact with worshippers' foreheads on row carpets. Silk and cotton were used to embellish parts of row carpets, adding beauty and richness, along with the soft silky feel. These materials are smoother and easier to adapt to the decorative shape required. Using linen to create the outer edge of row carpets helped protect and preserve the decorations in the interior space. The outer edges were woven in sturdy threads of linen to prolong the carpet's life span, also making it easy to move, fold and furnish. Edges are the most vulnerable part of the carpet, and this practical solution created a protective frame using more durable materials.

To create row carpets such as this one, the carpet maker would pull the vertical warp threads and the horizontal weft threads firmly and tightly, then weave the threads according to the design prepared in advance by the senior designer. Afterwards, the carpet maker would refine the design using manual tools, such as knives, scissors, combs and hooks.

Islamic carpets are generally made with vertical and horizontal looms, but row carpets in particular were created using a wide horizontal loom to help the carpet maker produce the final shape of the carpet with adjacent and horizontally aligned niches. The carpet maker would have the design on a paper sketch in front of him as he implemented it.

Carpet makers would make and decorate row carpets from right to left, using dyed and colored threads prepared in advance to add the number of niches required to decorate the row carpet, as agreed between the head of the workshop and the carpet maker. The looms were relatively sophisticated, allowing them to create both the carpet and decorations simultaneously, unlike simple looms used to create early carpets prior to row carpets, or those with simpler decoration.

The carpet maker used the Turkish knot (also called Ghiordes, full knot, double knot or symmetric knot), to create the pile of this part of the row carpet. In the Ghiordes knot, the weft yarn passes over the two warp yarns, and is pulled through between them and then cut to form the pile, making it firm and durable. This knot is often used in prayer rugs and row carpets. To create densely packed decorative motifs requires a strong knot intricately woven on warp yarns, and also entails large numbers of knots per inch, which is estimated in this part of the carpet as being 106 full knots in every square inch (2.5 × 2.5 cm). Impressively, the carpet maker took into account the space allocated for each worshipper on the row carpet before and during the manufacturing process.

In this Ushak row carpet, which measures 80 × 153 cm, the niche space dedicated to each individual completely matches the space needed to stand, kneel, prostrate themselves or perform prayer movements. We can see that the width between the two ends below the niche – the space dedicated for worshippers to stand – is 80 cm, which is indeed the most suitable space for the worshipper to stand and pray. The length provides the perfect space for the worshipper as he kneels, prostrates himself and sits.

The artist evenly distributed the symmetrical ornaments below the niche arch and on both its sides. By performing calculations and measurements in advance, and applying the rules of geometry, the artist achieved this wonderful harmony. When the artist created the decorative design, he had to calculate the required number of threads and knots to create each ornament. Then, he calculated the number of decorative elements required to fill the space in each ornament of the row carpet. The artist made all the calculations before manufacturing the carpet, or even pulling the threads on the loom, as there is no room for improvisation.

Row carpets are divided into identical and evenly vertical compartments. In this section of the row carpet, we find 56 flowers which are perfectly aligned on both sides of the niche and the bukhari ornament beneath the arch. Precision and concentration are required in calculating the number of threads and knots, while taking into account the structural proportions of ornamentation, especially since all these decorations were hand-knotted.

Using natural vegetal and animal dyes for the yarns, the artist ensured an overall harmony of color in the different shades of red and blue. Thus, the ornaments and motifs were contrasted by combining light and dark colors,

9.5 **Textile**
This wall textile contains a row of four arches, in each of which hangs a mosque lamp containing a mirror image of the Arabic inscription: "He (Allah) is the Remaining, the Living Almighty." This type of textile was probably used to indicate the qibla rather than to pray on.

Turkey, 15th–16th century
Silk with silver thread
Length: 115 cm, Height: 66 cm
Museum of Islamic Art, Cairo 12014

with carpet decorations often appearing in bright colors against a dark background. Combining warm colors, such as red and orange, with cool colors, such as shades of blue, suggests several meanings. The transition from warm colors to cool colors in row carpets can suggest a moving inwards towards what is profound and spiritual. The color contrast also brings about a state of contemplation, especially as each color or colored motif is associated with certain objects or memories. The colors for this textile may have been chosen for their subliminal effect on people, and the meanings they generate.

Aesthetic and symbolic aspects

The philosophy of beauty and perfection was naturally acquired by Muslim craftsmen who grew up learning from the Holy Qur'an and Hadiths of the Prophet (ﷺ). They knew perfectly well the words of Allah the Almighty: "O children of Adam, take your adornment at every masjid, and eat and drink, but be not excessive. Indeed, He likes not those who commit excess" (Surat Al-A'raf, 7:31). They were also aware of Allah's words: "The mosques of Allah are only to be maintained by those who believe in Allah and the

Last Day and establish prayer and give zakah and do not fear except Allah, for it is expected that those will be of the [rightly] guided" (Surat At-Tawbah, 9:18). Additionally, they read and learned the Hadiths of the Prophet, in which he urged Muslims to embrace beauty and perfection, including the well-known Hadith where the Prophet says: "Allah is beautiful and He loves beauty" (Related by Sahih Muslim).

Therefore, row carpets should be understood as integral products of the collective Muslim society of their time, and representative of aesthetic and religious values in the Islamic community as a whole. When creating row carpets, the artist knows that he is making a religious masterpiece which serves social and charitable purposes, and will be used by all segments of society. Ushak row carpets may also contain subtle meanings, transporting the viewer to a world of wonder and beauty. As the viewer savors the elements of beauty in row carpets, he may grasp the implicit philosophical and symbolic aspects, proving that art is a living philosophy.

For example, the overall shape of row carpets refers to unity between Muslims, who pray in aligned rows similar to the rows of angels (Sahih Muslim). When being merciful, caring and compassionate, Muslims resemble one body and one heart.

Distributing the ornaments in aligned and symmetrical shapes was a proof of the artist's accuracy, order and commitment. This can be seen as relating to the order and regularity of the five daily prayers, which are held at specific times, and performed in a precise order.

9.6 **Prayer Rug**
This typical late Ottoman prayer rug was probably used by its owner both in mosques and during travel. Consequently, these rugs would be carried vast distances and were often found in places far from their original place of manufacture.

Turkey, 18th century
Wool pile
Height: 177 cm, Width: 127 cm
Museum of Islamic Art, Cairo 15776

Niches are used in row carpets to point in the direction of qibla. They also convey several symbolic and philosophical meanings. The niche is the heart of the mosque and is considered its most important part. It represents the qibla for worshippers. Therefore, it is a symbol of both the mosque and the prayers.

The lamp hanging from the niche relates to prayers and their spiritual effect in the heart of worshippers. The word *mishkah* (mosque lamp or niche) means a closed hatch in the wall, which is the place dedicated for keeping the lamp. *Mishkahs* symbolize the divine light, as Allah the Almighty says: "The example of His light is like a niche within which is a lamp ..." (Surat Al-Nur, 24:35).

The bukharia echoes the decoration commonly found on Holy Qur'an covers inside the mosque, as well as the doors through which worshippers enter the mosque to stand on the row carpet to pray.

Botanical motifs on row carpets combine elegance and decorative beauty, as well as realism and closeness to nature. As such, the artist invites viewers of row carpets to reflect on the magnificent creations made by Allah the Almighty. Clove flowers have been understood as symbolizing happiness and wisdom in the Turkic-speaking world, while tulips symbolize success, love and spirituality. The name for tulip in Turkish is "lale" and evokes similar sounds to the word "Allah".

Geometric ornaments partially represent the philosophy of commitment, using abstract geometric lines in precise mathematical proportions and in regular repetition. The carpet is used by worshippers to perform five prayers every day and night. This daily recurrence and everlasting nature of prayers match the philosophy of repeated geometric shapes used in row carpets.

Conclusion

At the end of this short and profound journey through time, we see how the row carpet has been a key part of the mosque, encapsulating the whole. It displays unique qualities of Islamic art: gathering the whole in the part, and presenting the part as an independent decorative unit, yet inseparable from the whole.

This row carpet is a work of art which combines beauty and function, without one element overshadowing the other. It is a symbol of faith and beauty, evoking delight and joy in the heart of worshippers. Row carpets combined elements of design, color and texture in harmony. Each section of a row carpet is a symbol of the mosque, embodying all its artistic and architectural features, thanks to the ornamentation urging the worshippers to turn towards the Grand Mosque of Makkah. As they stand on a row carpet which combined beauty, imagination and perfection, they know with absolute certainty that Allah is beautiful and He loves beauty.

9.7 **Prayer Rug**
Colored blue with indigo dye, this unique prayer rug features the *mihrab* niche element and two columns echoing the architecture of the mosque.

Turkey or Egypt, 18th century
Wool pile
Height: 155 cm, Width: 110 cm
Museum of Islamic Art, Cairo 15815

9.8 **Prayer Rug**
The existence of various types and designs of prayer rugs can be explained by the distinct styles that were created over time in villages and smaller towns across Turkey. This example is from Milas, in western Turkey, which was particularly famous for its textile production.

Milas, Turkey, 19th century
Wool pile
Height: 133 cm, Width: 107 cm
Museum of Islamic Art, Cairo 15818

9.9 **Prayer Rug**

This prayer rug, or *sejjadah* in Arabic, was among the most popular textiles woven in Turkey. Common features are the characteristic niche design evoking the *mihrab* (prayer niche) and the smaller size that makes such carpets suitable for individual use.

Turkey, 17th century
Wool pile
Height: 200 cm, Width: 120 cm
Museum of Islamic Art, Cairo 15809

10 Reflections on the *Minbar*

Minwer al-Meheid

In 1969, to widespread dismay, the *minbar* (pulpit) of Saladin, which had stood for 800 years in Jerusalem's Al-Aqsa Mosque, Islam's third holiest site, was tragically destroyed following a devastating fire. The pulpit was commissioned in the middle of the 12th century by Nur ad-Din Mahmud ibn Zengi, and moved to its place in Al-Aqsa Mosque following Saladin's recapturing of Jerusalem. The intricately designed and crafted wooden pulpit was widely considered one of the greatest masterpieces of Islamic art for its detailed craftsmanship and elegant design. Contemporaries lavished praise on it, with the famous 12th-century traveler Ibn Jubayr pronouncing the pulpit as beautiful "beyond description."

The restoration of the Al-Aqsa Mosque and *minbar* was a difficult and arduous task. Those responsible grappled with questions as to how to restore and rebuild the mosque, as well as how to replace Saladin's *minbar*.

10.1 **The Reconstructed *Minbar* of Saladin in the Al-Aqsa Mosque** After years of painstaking reconstruction work by Dr. Minwer al-Meheid and a team of international craftsmen, the *minbar* of Saladin was reinstalled in Jerusalem's Al-Aqsa Mosque in 2006.

10.2 **Saladin's *Minbar* (Pulpit) in the Al-Aqsa Mosque, Jerusalem** This black-and-white photograph, dating from the early 20th century, shows Saladin's *minbar* before the fire of 1969. The Al-Aqsa Mosque is regarded by Muslims as the third-holiest mosque after Makkah and Medina.

Should there be a replica of the original *minbar* or a completely new and contemporary work of art? The crux of the question was that,

> on the one hand, the *minbar* was irreplaceable – it was a relic of a bygone age, a physical link with the glorious past, an object that had 800 years of history layered into its being. No matter what was put in its place, nothing else could claim these unique qualities. On the other hand, it was precisely these qualities that made its complete erasure such a depressing prospect. An entirely new, totally different modern work would simply emphasize the loss. The inevitable conclusion was that because of its iconic status and significance, the new *minbar* should replicate the old one. It would be made of the same methods and from the finest materials and by the most outstanding craftsmen. It should be as though Saladin's *minbar* had risen from the ashes, precise in every detail.
> (Singer. 2008, 63)

Thus, 30 years following its tragic loss, I answered an international call for design submissions announced by King Hussein of Jordan to reconstruct the famous pulpit. In the months that followed, I devoted myself to studying the pulpit's geometry and construction, of which only charred fragments remained. Moreover, since knowledge of its construction and complex geometric decoration was now lost and no longer practiced by Muslim craftsmen, I had to draw on my years of personal experience

10.3 **Al-Aqsa Mosque: Jerusalem**
Al-Aqsa (which means "the furthest") Mosque can be identified by its gray dome and represents the first qibla, or direction of prayer, for Muslims. Opposite stands the Dome of the Rock, with its golden cupola, marking the location from where Prophet Mohammed (ﷺ) began his miraculous Night Journey (*Mi'raj*) to Heaven.

and research into traditional geometry and construction techniques. My submission was ultimately successful and so I produced specifications for about 16,358 pieces, all of which needed to fit together without nails, screws or glue, into a harmonious and beautiful whole that exactly replicated its illustrious predecessor.

Reconstructing the *minbar* from scratch was a Herculean task, more so because of the lack of the necessary expertise and the loss of the secrets of its original making and design. I directed a handpicked team of international master craftsmen who reconstructed the pulpit using traditional techniques, materials and methods of construction. The process of reconstructing this jewel of Islamic art also led me on a personal journey deep into layers of history to discover the meanings behind the pulpit, leading ultimately to the original pulpit that once stood in the Prophet's (ﷺ) Mosque in Medina.

Definition and function

Unlike other distinct features of mosques, such as the *mihrab* (prayer niche) and minaret (the tower from where the call for prayer was performed) which were introduced after the Prophet Mohammed's (ﷺ) death, the *minbar* was fashioned and used during his lifetime. Indeed, the pulpit has been an essential element in mosques since the earliest establishment of the Islamic community in Medina. A *minbar* normally comprises a raised platform in the front area of a mosque, from which sermons or speeches are given. The pulpit is located to the right of the *mihrab*, which marks the direction of the qibla for prayer. Hadiths of the Prophet (ﷺ) mention the various virtues of the pulpit, giving it an important status in Islam as it was considered an essential and organic element of the mosque. Pulpits were closely related to preaching, which was the cornerstone of congregational prayers on Fridays and both 'Id festivals. Additionally, pulpits were the symbol of Muslim rule and the most important official emblem signifying the religious, political and social unity of Islam. The fact that the pulpit was used during the time of the Prophet provided his successors, the caliphs, with a powerful endorsement and the *minbar* came to be viewed as a symbol of authority.

The origin of the word commonly used for pulpit, *minbar*, is *nabara*, which refers to height, elevation or an object which has more qualities than other

10.4 **The Interior of the 14th-century Sultan Hassan Mosque in Cairo**
A quintessential mosque scene: An inlaid stone and marble *minbar* is seen alongside the *mihrab* (prayer niche), above which are suspended numerous mosque lamps.

similar objects. The *minbar* is usually made of carved wood (although examples are also found in stone, alabaster or brick) and comprises a short staircase leading to the top platform, which is sometimes covered by a small canopy. In addition to making the speaker visible to worshippers, the pulpit helped to amplify the voice of the speaker across the prayer hall before the use of microphones. Traditional *minbars* are considered a common element in Islamic mosque architecture all over the world, and are made in various sizes and boast various decorations.

Historically, caliphs, sultans and rulers utilized these pulpits to deliver sermons in fulfillment of their duty of the caliphate. Additionally, they have been used by preachers to deliver sermons throughout Islamic history.

The Berber *minbar*

This beautiful yet elegantly simple pulpit (Figure 10.5) is rare and uniquely special, because of its date and origin. It was made sometime in the mid-1700s and originally belonged in a small, local Friday congregational mosque in one of the many Berber villages or towns scattered across the foothills of the Atlas Mountains. The pulpit, made from Atlas cedar and joined with iron nails, has three steps, a seat and an entrance porch surmounted by an elaborate crest. The elements of the main body are assembled from rectangular panels engraved and painted with geometric motifs enhanced with dark orange and black pigments. An interesting tradition that became distinctive of pulpits in North Africa, such as this one, was their mobility. In North Africa and Muslim Spain, it became common practice to store the pulpit in a closet built into the wall to the right of the *mihrab*. Because they were quite heavy, Maghribi pulpits, like this one, were built on wheels so that they could be rolled out of the storage, and wooden tracks were often laid on the carpets or mats of the mosque floor to make the task easier.

Each of the pulpit's four stair risers shows the common motif of horseshoe arches (Figure 10.6), in addition to the elegant pointed horseshoe arch that opens before the steps, echoing earlier pulpits on which this one was based. Indeed, the models for this kind of pulpit go back to the grand Almoravid pulpit commissioned for the Kutubiyya Mosque in Marrakech (see Figure 10.8), Morocco, and the Great Mosque of Cordoba, Spain, both of which are believed to have been made in the same Spanish workshop

10.5 **Berber *Minbar***
Originally located in a small Friday mosque in the Atlas Mountains, this *minbar* was modeled on earlier Berber examples, such as the grand Almoravid *minbar* in the Kutubiyya Mosque in Marrakech (built 1137). As such, it harkens back to their golden age when Berber tribes ruled large parts of Morocco and Spain.

Berber, Morocco, Middle Atlas Mountains, 18th century
Painted cedar wood joined with iron nails
Height: 158 cm, Depth: 60 cm; door arch height: 215 cm
Ithra Museum 2019.0060

in Cordoba sometime during the 12th century. The *minbar* from the Kutubiyya Mosque, still extant and on view at the Dar al-Batha Museum in Marrakech, was commissioned by the last Almoravid sultan, Ali ibn Yusuf, for his congregational mosque in 1137. Ethnically Berber, the Almoravid dynasty (al-Murabitun, c. 1062–1150) ruled large parts of North Africa and Spain and were known for their piety and the austerity in which they led their lives, closely following the example of the Prophet (ﷺ). This characteristic is often reflected in their early art and architecture which is notable for its simple and austere use of decoration. For example, the Kutubiyya *minbar* – considered a national treasure of Morocco – despite incorporating intricately inlaid and carved wood panels including costly materials, has an undeniable restrained beauty and elegance about it. This beauty ultimately found expression in the *minbar* seen before us, hence why I view this Berber *minbar* as an embodiment of the *minbars* of the great Berbers who ruled huge swathes of the Sahara, Morocco, Algeria and Spain since the 11th century.

10.6 **Detail on the Berber *Minbar***
Perhaps echoing the *mihrab* niche or the archways within the mosque where it once stood, this *minbar*'s stair risers are painted with the typical Moroccan horseshoe arch motif.

The *minbar*, a historical background

The earliest pulpit of this type can be linked to the Prophet's (ﷺ) Mosque in Medina. After the Prophet (ﷺ) moved to Medina from Makkah in 622, the Muslim community began to grow at a fast pace and the Prophet (ﷺ) consequently needed to be seen and heard over greater distances as he addressed an expanding congregation. Various Hadiths and historical accounts describe objects that can be considered the precursor of the Prophet Mohammed's (ﷺ) pulpit in Medina. The first of these precursors was during the early days of Hijra when a *dakkah*, or raised platform of clay, was constructed on which the Prophet used to sit. This would distinguish him to visitors and it was also the place from which he used to deliver his sermon on Fridays. These same accounts also indicate that the Prophet delivered his Friday sermons (khutbahs) while leaning on a dry palm tree trunk fixed in the ground. This palm trunk was known as *Al Mukhalaqa* or *Al Mutaiba* and was scented with *teeb* or perfume. Later, at the request of the Prophet (ﷺ), a young carpenter, the son of a revered Muslim woman companion from Al Ansar, made the first wooden pulpit in Islam from tamarisk wood sometime during the seventh or eighth year after Hijra. Ibn al-Najjar described the pulpit by saying: "The Prophet's pulpit measured two cubits (approx. 120 cm) in height, one cubit by one cubit (approx. 60 × 60 cm) in width, and had two finials, each with a height of half a cubit (30 cm), upon which the Prophet used to rest his two honorable hands when seated." (*Khulaset al-Wafa Bi Akhbar Dar al-Mustafa*, V2, 162–4).

When delivering the sermon, Prophet Mohammed (ﷺ) used to sit on the upper third step, putting his honorable feet on the second step of this pulpit. This pulpit was subsequently placed on the west side (right

10.7 **Berber town in the Atlas Mountains**
The Berber town and Mosque of Tinghir in the Todra Valley in the Middle Atlas Mountains of Morocco. It has been recorded that by the mid-eighth century, during the Abbasid period, there were *minbars* in every city that had a congregational mosque.

10.8 **The Interior of the Kutubiyya Mosque, Marrakech, Morocco**
The elegantly simple arcades of the Kutubiyya Mosque impress with their repetition and restrained elegance. The great Berber dynasties – the Almohads and Almoravids – tended to avoid excessive ornamentation and this is evident in their art and architecture, even influencing later Berber art, such as the Berber *minbar* in question (Figure 10.5).

side) of the *mihrab*, which was indicated with a black stone, inside the Prophet's (ﷺ) Mosque in Medina. The pulpit's backrest was formed by three wooden boards (two uprights and a crossbar), and its arms ended in finials, over which the Prophet (ﷺ) would rest his hands. The Prophet (ﷺ) used the pulpit to deliver Friday sermons, to speak about community matters and to answer queries from the members of the congregation. In fact, the informal attitude of the Prophet (ﷺ) to the pulpit is confirmed by reports that he used to sit on it for impromptu gatherings while his listeners squatted on the ground around him.

There are a few interesting stories in the Hadith concerning the pulpit of the Prophet (ﷺ). When the Prophet (ﷺ) started to use the newly made pulpit, the trunk on which he used to lean began to cry like a she-camel, so the Prophet (ﷺ) descended from his seat and put his honorable hands on it until it calmed down (Sahih Bukhari). Another pertains to one of the few instances in which Prophet Mohammed (ﷺ) is mentioned as praying (*Dua'*) from the pulpit. In one instance, he said a prayer invoking rain (*salat al-Istisqa*) from the pulpit, and it rained so heavily for a week that the following Friday he had to pray again to stop further rainfall and flooding (Sahih Bukhari).

This pulpit remained in its original state during the reign of the Rashidun caliphs (may Allah be pleased with them) who continued to use it when delivering sermons and announcements. Caliph Abu Bakr Al Siddiq (may Allah be pleased with him) sat on the second step, placing his feet on the first step, while Caliph Omar ibn Al Khattab (may Allah be pleased with him), sat on the first step, placing his feet on the ground. Caliph Uthman ibn Affan (may Allah be pleased with him) sat on the lower step for six years, and then rose to where the Prophet used to stand and deliver sermons. In the Maghreb, this tradition was closely followed under the Maliki School (jurisprudence) where the *khatib* (preacher) would only ascend to the middle step, not to the top, and would remain standing, since only Prophet Mohammed (ﷺ) and the first caliphs had the privilege of sitting on the pulpit. This tradition evokes the respect shown to the Prophet (ﷺ) by his companions.

During the caliphate of Muawiyah, which followed the reign of the Rightly Guided Caliphs, the governor of Medina, Marwan Ibn al-Hakam, added six steps made of ebony to the base of the pulpit, which resulted in a new eight-step pulpit that was much more imposing. It was

10.9 **The Ninth-Century Mosque of Ibn Tulun in Cairo**
The central courtyard seen from inside the prayer hall shows the distinctive water fountain (sabil) with a high drum dome, added at the end of the 13th century, and the spiral minaret which was constructed in the Samarran style common in Abbasid constructions in Iraq.

formalized as the seat of state and religion before it slowly acquired its definitive character as a pulpit used only for the Friday sermon in mosques.

About 50 years after the death of the Prophet (ﷺ), the main mosque in the capital of every province of the Islamic caliphate had its own pulpit, which was supposedly built according to the original model in Medina. The first wooden pulpit to be placed in a mosque, other than the Prophet's (ﷺ) Mosque, is attributed to Amr ibn Al 'As when he governed Egypt under the caliphate of Omar ibn Al Khattab (may Allah be pleased with him). He planned the city of Fustat, where he established a mosque and ordered for a pulpit to be created and placed inside the mosque in 641. Later, Caliph Muawiyah ibn Abi Sufyan was the first to introduce the pulpit to the Great Mosque of Makkah. He commissioned the construction of a portable wooden pulpit, which was placed next to the Ka'ba, to deliver sermons. His son Yazid, the second Umayyad caliph, also established a mosque with a pulpit in Jund Qansrin. Al Hajjaj ibn Yusuf Al Thaqafi, the governor of Iraq under the Umayyad Caliph Abdul Malik ibn Marwan, also used to deliver sermons from the pulpit of the Great Mosque of Kufa. The Umayyad interest in establishing *minbars* inside mosques continued until 749, when Caliph Marwan bin Muhammad ordered the ruler of Egypt, Musa ibn Nusayr, to "take pulpits to the villages," i.e. to place a pulpit in the congregational mosque of each major city. Thus, *minbar* became an integral element of congregational mosques. Most, if not all, mosques in the Muslim world have pulpits, the most famous of which is the striking one in the Mosque of Ibn Tulun in Egypt (Figures 10.9 and 10.10). Thus, by the mid-eighth century, during the Abbasid period, there were pulpits in every city that had a congregational mosque. The geographer al-Muqaddasi (d. 1000) wrote that "a town is so designated if it has a pulpit (i.e. a congregational mosque)."

Meanwhile, the pulpit of the Prophet (ﷺ) stood in his mosque for around 600 years, only succumbing to a fire in the 13th century. During this time, the pulpit became a permanent reminder of his blessed presence and many visitors and travelers wrote moving accounts of it. The fires which erupted in this mosque seem to have made Muslims consider using a more resistant and longer-lasting material than wood to create pulpits, with some opting for marble or alabaster. The first pulpit of this type was sent by Sultan Al Ashraf Qaitbay to replace the

second replacement wooden pulpit of the Prophet's (ﷺ) Mosque, which perished in the second fire. It was made of white marble. This was followed by a pulpit sent by the Ottoman Sultan Murad III in 1598. This immensely beautiful and meticulously crafted *minbar* was made of pure alabaster and was the last pulpit to be placed in the Prophet's (ﷺ) Mosque, where it still stands and is used to deliver sermons.

Meaning and symbol

There is a very special quality about the Berber *minbar*; the object wears its history on its sleeve, and its beautiful worn and darkened patina shows the wear and tear of time. Its removal from its original mosque has clearly taken its toll. The effect of the reflected light from the mosque windows glittering on the dark depths of the painted wood would have been an astonishing sight to behold.

Like the great monumental pulpits commissioned by the Berber sultans and leaders and installed in great Friday mosques of capital cities like Cordoba and Marrakech, this Berber pulpit, which occupied a corner in a small congregational mosque in the foothills of the Atlas on the margins of the Islamic empire, had an important purpose for those people it served. It was from this pulpit that their local imam would deliver the Friday sermon. It may have also functioned as the seat from where their teachers would instill in the young the words of God and the deeds and actions of the blessed Prophet (ﷺ). This object represents the intermediary role of the imam or the khatib, and commemorates the actions and legacy of Prophet Mohammed (ﷺ). While the Berber *minbar* presented here takes inspiration from the grand Berber *minbars* of old, in terms of its small size, modest construction and elegantly simple use of ornamentation, it is more evocative of the Prophet's pulpit than any I have seen before.

Finally, as a historical artifact, it is charged with meaning and historical significance, not of great conquerors or leaders that changed the course of history, but of small communities living out their lives with dignity and beauty.

10.10 **The Interior of the Mosque of Ibn Tulun in Cairo**
A wooden *minbar* is seen alongside the *mihrab*.

Appendix

Author Biographies

Abdullah H. Alkadi (chapter 1)

Prof. Abdullah Alkadi, is vice-president for Development, Studies and Communication Services at Imam Abdulrahman Bin Faisal University (University of Dammam) and professor of Urban and Regional Planning. He completed his doctorate in 1996 at Portland State University, Oregon. He is also an architect, urban planner and historian and has authored

numerous books and articles focusing on early Islamic history and civilization, with a particular focus on the Hijaz. Prof. Alkadi has been praised internationally for his pioneering research on the various travel routes by the Prophet Mohammed (ﷺ) and his companions. His groundbreaking book *Makkah to Medina: A Photographic Journey of the Hijrah Route* is widely considered one of the most significant studies coming from a Saudi scholar in a generation. He regularly tours the world to promote his work and share his research.

Sami Angawi (chapter 2)

Dr. Sami Angawi is the founder and director of the Hajj Research Center, which he established in 1975. He was also the founder and general director of the Amar Center for Architecture. He supervises in areas of architectural design, planning, conservation, restoration and development of traditional architectural heritage, research and documentation of traditional architecture. In 2011, he designed the Al-Makkiyah Al-Madaniyah Institute, taking traditional Makkan architecture and Islamic architectural traditions worldwide. He is a fellow of the Harvard Graduate School of Design and a former associate member of

Harvard University's Semitic Museum for Consultation on Historic Architecture and Arts of Arabia. Dr. Angawi has a PhD in Philosophy in Islamic Architecture from London's School of Oriental and African Studies and a Master of Architecture and Urban Studies from the University of Texas, Austin.

Raeda Ashour (chapter 4)

Saudi Arabian artist Raeda Ashour specializes in miniatures, motifs and Islamic decorative units, adapting them in a modern style. Characteristics of her work include harmonious variance in surface treatment, hand-embossing and soft colors. Before returning to Saudi Arabia in 1991,

she lived in Cairo, where she worked in publishing. She has a BA in Middle East Studies from the American University of Cairo. In 2007, she received a MA in Arts Education from Rushmore University, an online institution, and attended workshops in Islamic Illumination at the Prince's Foundation School of Traditional Arts in London in 2014. She has showcased her artworks in more than 50 collective exhibitions, such as Saudi Cultural Week in Moscow in 2007 and 2017, Dolmabahce Gallery, Istanbul, and the Saudi Women Artists' Exhibition at UNESCO-Beirut in 2001. She has also held solo exhibitions across the Middle East, including Jeddah, Kuwait and Cairo.

Lisa Delong (chapter 6)
Dr. Lisa DeLong studied painting and received her MA in Art History at Brigham Young University, Provo, Utah. She moved to London in 2001, where she studied with Professor Keith Critchlow and Paul Marchant, two of the world's foremost geometers. She completed her doctoral studies at London's Prince's Foundation School of Traditional Arts in 2007. Her first book, *Curves: Flowers, Foliates and Flourishes in the Formal Decorative Arts*, was published in November 2013 and reviewed in the *New York Times*. In 2016, she presented a TEDx talk on geometry and education. Dr. DeLong is now Outreach Program Manager for the Prince's School, designing and conducting educational programs internationally. In her paintings, she investigates the beauty found in the conversation between order and the unexpected, chaos and cosmos. Both the patterns and the raw materials of her paintings are informed by her travels and research with the School of Traditional Arts.

Mohammed Abdel Bari (chapter 7)
Mohammed Abdel Bari is a noted Sudanese poet, writer and intellectual who specializes in the areas of philosophy and thought. He is at the forefront of the current wave of contemporary Arabic poets. His poetry deals with mystical, philosophical, political and subjective dimensions, with a modernistic-heritage tendency that belongs to the spaces of contemplation, introspection and intuition. In composing his poetry, he uses various cultural influences and a profound knowledge of the depths of the human soul. He has become well known and recognized in the Arab world. He has won multiple poetry awards and honors, such as the Prince Abdullah Al Faisal International Prize for Arabic Poetry (2019), the African Arab Youth Award (2016) and Sharjah Award for Arab Creativity (2013).

Oludamini Ogunnaike (chapter 8)
Prof. Oludamini Ogunnaike is a scholar of Islamic, African and religious studies, with a focus on the intellectual and artistic dimensions of Sufism and Ifa, an indigenous Yoruba religious tradition. His work examines the postcolonial, colonial and precolonial Islamic and indigenous religious traditions of North and West Africa. He holds a BA in Cognitive Neuroscience and African Studies from Harvard College, an MA and PhD in African Studies and Religious Studies from Harvard University, and spent a year as a postdoctoral fellow at Stanford's Abbasi Program in Islamic Studies. He served as an assistant professor of Islamic Studies at the College of William & Mary in Williamsburg, Virginia, for three years, and now teaches at the University of Virginia, in Charlottesville, as an assistant professor of African Religious Thought. He is completing work on two book manuscripts: *Deep Knowledge: Ways of Knowing in Sufism and Ifa: Two West African Intellectual Traditions* (Penn State University Press) and *Poetry in Praise of Prophetic*

Perfection: West African Arabic Madīḥ Poetry and its Precedents (Islamic Texts Society).

Mohamed Ahmed Abd el-Salam (chapter 9)

Dr. Mohamed Ahmed Mohamed Mohamed Abd el-Salam is deputy director of the Museum of Islamic Art in Cairo, where he is Curator of

the Textiles and Carpets Department. He holds a master's degree on the subject of Indian Mughal carpets and has a doctorate in Islamic Chinese arts and Chinese influences in Japanese and Korean art between the 16th and 19th centuries. He trained in museology at the British Museum in London and also at the Louvre in Paris, and also received scholarships for study in Germany and the UK. He also teaches Islamic arts and museology in Arabic, English and Persian.

Minwer al-Meheid (chapter 10)

Dr. Minwer al-Meheid is a highly accomplished project manager with a particular emphasis on architectural engineering and design. He started his varied career in 1983 as a project manager for

high-budget projects in Saudi Arabia and has continued with award-winning projects, most notably the reconstruction of the *minbar* of Salahuddin at Al-Aqsa Mosque in Jerusalem in 2007. He is also an accomplished academic, having established the College of Islamic Art and Architecture in Jordan. He continues to work in a professional capacity in Jordan, having worked on projects for the Royal Hashemite Court and the Jordanian Ministry of Endowments.

Acknowledgments

This book accompanies the exhibition *The Art of Orientation*. Neither could have been achieved without the help of a number of individuals and institutions across the world. It is our great pleasure to express our warmest thanks to them here.

First and foremost, we would like to thank our colleagues at Ithra who supported this project from its conception right the way through to its realization. Principal among them is our Head of Museums, Laila Al-Faddagh, Director of Programs Abdullah Al Rashid, former Division Head Abdullah Al Eyaf and Director Hussain N. Hanbazazah, as well as our General Manager, Fahad Al Dubaib, and our Vice-President, Nabil A. Nuaim. Quite simply, without their unstinting support, this exhibition would not have been possible. We would also like to acknowledge the tireless work of the Ithra's museum team, in particular those people who were directly involved in creating this exhibition, including project manager Paul Soderblom, head of exhibition design Young Kim and his team, Mai Al-Naimi and Dalia Al-Ghamdi, and the head of conservation and collections, Konstantinos Chatziantoniou, and his colleagues Alejandro R. Malinog Jr., Alejandro Bolina, Gregorio Fernandez, Jhuh Mercurio, Ricky Galavo, Judifel Valdez and Crisanto Amago.

Then there are those who supported us behind the scenes and to whom we owe a debt of gratitude, including Manar Aldhwila, Adrian Cross, Mishaal Alsarra, Mohammad Atta, Fahad Alfear and Mark Wright, Tariq Ahmad, John Wenzelberger, Norah Alrasheed, Patricia Lechner-Phua, Anthony Brookes and Ernesto Berger. All these people helped us navigate the challenges that come with organizing an international exhibition of this magnitude. There were also numerous people at Saudi Aramco Corporate Affairs, including Ismail S. Al-Dossary, Abdulwahed Abdulhameed Al-Makki and Fahad M. Albagmi. Our utmost gratitude goes to Saudi Aramco Government Affairs, including Rufyda Abdullatief Alabdalla, Falah A. Al-Otaibi, Omar AbdulAziz Al-Niaimi and Ibrahim Abdulaziz Al-Sanea. Special thanks to those who supported this exhibition through the facilitation of large amounts of paperwork, including, but not limited to, obtaining permissions to film in the Two Holy Mosques and facilitating official letters between the different parties and stakeholders involved in this international exhibition, including Sulaiman Aljared, Tarig Abuleef, Khalid Hussin AlKurdi, Adil A. Al-Ereinan, Abdulaziz G. Raheem, Mazin Abdulrazzaq Al-Fudhail, Ibrahim A. Bukhari, Abdullah A. Al Ghamdi, Abdullah A. AlFozan, Abdulmajeed AlAhmari and Mohammed Ibrahim Abu Theraa.

Many of the works included in this book and exhibition have traveled from the Museum of Islamic Art in Cairo (MIA) under the auspices of the Supreme Council of Egyptian Antiquities. We are enormously grateful to MIA and the Supreme Council for their generosity in sharing their collection for the benefit and edification of the Saudi public. In particular, we would like to express our gratitude to MIA Director Dr. Mamdouh Osman and the Head of Museums Sector at the Egyptian Ministry of Tourism & Antiquities, Dr. Moamen Othman, as well as all their colleagues who have supported this partnership between our institutions. Organizing such a large and high-profile loan from the world's largest, and most celebrated, Islamic art collection represents a major cultural achievement for our institution and we are deeply grateful to all those involved in bringing it to fruition. We are also immensely proud that this loan of Islamic artifacts from Egypt signals one of the first major partnership between Saudi and Egyptian museums to date. We are also deeply grateful to our colleagues Rustom M. Kubaisi, Mohammed A. Al-Ahmari, Majed A. Al-Hasnah and Moayad Abdulaziz Alsaleh at the National Museum in Riyadh, who loaned us several significant artifacts from their collection for this exhibition.

Aramco Overseas Company (AOC) gave generous and diligent support, acting on Ithra's behalf to agree this loan of Islamic artifacts with the Supreme Council of Egyptian Antiquities. It was largely the efforts of Talal Al Marry (CEO), Rusha K Rawaf, Abdullah Abdullah, Maarten Obbes, Ghada Salama and Munira Suwailem that made this possible.

Indeed, bringing these Islamic works to Ithra has been a fascinating journey and an enjoyable process of discovery and learning over a number of years. It started out with a visit by our museum head, Laila Al-Faddagh, to the Museum of Islamic Art in Cairo to meet with its illustrious director, Dr. Mamdouh Osman, and his colleague and senior curator Dr. Mohamed Abdelsalam. From the outset, their high degree of professionalism and commitment to making this partnership work has been heartwarming. We would therefore like to extend our deepest heartfelt thanks to them and all their colleagues at their museum who helped in preparing their collection for this exhibition.

Various other partners and individuals have given generously of their time and expertise to make this exhibition a success, including Professor Mashary A. Al Naim and Dr. Hani M. Al Huneidi of the Al-Fozan Mosque Award. We would also like to acknowledge the hugely important role played by Filmmaster MEA and their various partners, who all worked diligently to project manage, design and build this exhibition. In particular, we would like to thank project managers and coordinators Michael Depypere and his colleagues Amanda Abou Jaoude, Christophe Defrance and Damien Hubert, as well as Annesing's Eric Tan (expert model maker) and exhibition designer Matt Langstaff and graphic designer Andrew Galvin, photographers at Mad Production Maxime Casa and Xavier Ansart for the wonderful photographs contained in this catalogue. Finally, we are grateful to their colleagues at Fractal for their work in filming the interviews for the exhibition and the Virtual reality footage at mosque locations around the world; they include Till Louesse, Numan Jayasekara, Sameer Antulay and Mohamed Al Hamdani. They all went above and beyond what was asked of them and delivered on a very ambitious and complex project to a high degree of satisfaction.

Finally, this book could not have been written without our hardworking and talented editorial team of people both within Ithra and outside. Particularly notable amongst them are Mona Mansour, Murdo MacLeod and Eeman Juhani, who contributed extensively to this catalogue.

Their skill, intelligence, good cheer and hard work have been unfailing and we are hugely grateful to them. Others who helped prepare the catalogue include Jane Robson (copy editor), Mohammad Shaban (translator) and Gunnar Musan (book designer). However, most of all, it is our guest authors – Sami Angawi, Abdullah Alkadi, Minwer al-Meheid, Oludamini Ogunnaike, Raeda Ashour, Mohamed Abdelsalam, Lisa DeLong, Mohammed Abdel Bari – to whom we owe the largest debt of gratitude. For it is their work – rich, varied and thought-provoking – that has provided us with the most inspiration and food for thought. Their contributions found in this book are veritable goldmines of knowledge and insight and we are proud to have worked with them on this exposition on the mosque. This book represents a small testament to the work to which they have devoted their lives to exploring.

Idries Trevathan and Mona AlJalhami

Bibliography

Ad-Darsh, Sayed. "Wider Role of the Mosque as a Community Center (Part One): The Functions of the Prophet's Mosque". Viewed in October 2019. Retrieved from https://archive.islamonline.net/?p=5710.

Akkach, Samer, *Cosmology and Architecture in Premodern Islam: An Architectural Reading of Mystical Ideas*. Albany: State University of New York Press, 2005.

Al-Bukhari. Viewed in October 2019. Retrieved from: https://sunnah.com/bukhari 2019

Alexander, Christopher. *A Foreshadowing of 21st Century Art, the Color and Geometry of Very Early Turkish Carpets.* New York: Oxford University Press, 1993.

Alhamzah, Khalid A. *Late Mamluk Patronage.* Boca Raton: Universal-Publishers, 2009

"Qansuh al-Ghuri's Waqfs and His Foundations in Cairo." Ibid.

Al-Dawadari, Abu Bakr. Kanz al-durar wa-jami' al-ghurar. Qism al-Dirasat al-Islamiyah, al-Ma'had al-Almani lil-Athar bi-al-Qahirah. Beyrut; Wiesbaden. Kommission bei F. Steiner-Verlag. 1960.

Alkadi, Abdullah. *Makkah to Madinah: A Photographic Journey of the Hijrah Route*. Orient East Publishers. 2013

"A Examination of the Shift in Orientation from East to North as a Contemporary Geographical Reference: the Time, the Way and the Impact." *Journal of Al Madinah Al Munawarah Research and Studies Center,* 19 (2006): 213–64.

"Place and Time: Tracing of Milestones of the Prophet's Migration Route within Narratives of Scholars from 101–1339 AH Using Techniques of Quantative and Diagramic Analysis." *Journal of Al Madinah Al Munawarah Research and Studies Center* (2010) 33.

"Maps of the Prophet's Migration Routes: A Tracing and Analytical Study of Former Graphical Attempts." *The Scientific Journal of King Faisal University, Basic and Applied Science* (2011): 2.

"Production of the First Digital Map including all Landmarks of the Prophetic Migration Using GPS and Geographic Information System (GIS)." *The Journal of King Saud University, Division of Architecture and Planning* (2012): 24.

"Proposed Mechanism for Using Historical Maps in Pursuing Heritage Landmarks Sites on Modern Digital Maps Using Informatics Technologies: Al Madinah Al Munawarah Case Study." *The Scientific Journal of King Abdulaziz University: Basic and Applied Science,* 14 (2012): 1.

"Concept of Geographic Directions in the Holy Qur'an: Field Applications on Events Mentioned in the Quran and the Prophetic Biography." *The Scientific Journal of King Abdulaziz University*. (2012)

"Discovery of Milestones on the Caravan Road from Makkah to Madinah using International Monitoring Systems and Geographic Information Systems (GPS)." *The Scientific Journal of King Khalid University.* (2012)

Al-Kuli, Ali Muhammad Al-Shadhili. *Dawr al masajid al-tarikhi fi al-Ilmi*, Cairo: Wazarat al-Awkaf, 1961.

Al-Maqrizi, Ahmad Ibn Ali. *Al-Mawaiz wa Alitibar fi dhikr al-Khitat wa-Al-athar*. Edited by Ahmed Ali al-Mulaiji. Beirut: Dar al Urfan. 1959.

Al-Hassani, Salim T. S. *1001 Inventions: the Enduring Legacy of Muslim Civilization*. Washington, D.C.: National Geographic Museum. 2012

Al-Sayyed Muhammad Khalifa Hammad. "Mihrab" in *Discover Islamic Art*, Museum with No Frontiers, 2019. *http://islamicart.museumwnf.org/database_item.php?id=object;ISL;eg;Mus01;42;en.Source*

Amin, Muhammad Muhammad. *Al Awkaf wa-l-hayah al-ijtimah'iya fi Misr, 648–923 H., 1250–1517 M: dirasa tarikhiya watha'iqiya.* Cairo: Dar al-Nadhda al-Arabiya, 1980.

"'Watha'iq waqf al-Sultan Qalawun 'ala al-Bimaristan al-Mansuri." Published as appendix in Ibn Habib, *Tadhkirat al-nabih fi ayyam al-Mansur wa banih*, vol. 1, 295–396. Cairo: al-Hay'a al-Misyiya al-'Amma li-li-Kitab, 1976–86.

ArtFundUK. *Art gives same level of pleasure as being in love* [video file]. Retrieved from https://www.youtube.com/watch?v=D_5twGr9l_0. 2011

Askari, Abdul Hamid Akhund and Nasreen. *Tale of the Tile: The Ceramic Traditions of Pakistan*. Karachi: Mohatta Palace Museum, 2011.

Aslanapa, Oktay. *One Thousand Years of Turkish Carpets.* Istanbul, Muhittin Salih Eren, 1988.

Azzam, Khaled, ed. *Arts and Crafts of the Islamic Lands*. London: Thames and Hudson. 2013.

Berkey, J. *The Transmission of knowledge in Medieval Cairo*. Princeton: Princeton University Press, 1992.

Barry, Michael. *Colour and Symbolism in Islamic Architecture: Eight Centuries of the Tile-Maker's Art*. London: Thames and Hudson Ltd. 1996.

Beyazıt, Deniz. "Ka'ba tile". *Aga Khan Museum*. Retrieved from https://www.agakhanmuseum.org/collection/artifact/tile-akm587. 2014

Bierman, Irene et al. "Ottoman art". Asian. Retrieved from https://education.asianart.org/explore-resources/background-information/ottoman-art.

Bloom, Jonathan. *The Grove Encyclopedia of Islamic Art and Architecture.* vol. 1–3. OUP USA, 2009

Bloom, Jonathan and Blair, Sheila, eds. *God is the Light of the Heaven and the Earth. Light in Islamic Art and Culture.* New Haven: Yale University Press. 2015

Bolwerk, A., Mack-Andrick, J., Lang, F. R., Dörfler, A. & Maihöfner, C. "How art changes your brain: Differential effects of visual art production and cognitive art evaluation on functional brain connectivity". *PLOS ONE* 9(7), 1–8. 2014

Breck, Joseph and Morris, Frances. *The James F. Ballard Collection of Oriental Rugs.* New York: the Metropolitan Museum of Art, 1923.

Burckhardt, Titus. *The Art of Islam: Language and Meaning*, Bloomington, World Wisdom, 2009.

Central Asian Art. London: Greenwich Editions, 2003.

Critchlow, Keith. VITA first year geometry background paper no. 1, 18 October 2002.

Critchlow, Keith and Marchant, Paul, "Zillij: A Geometric Analysis" in S. Samar Damluji, ed. *Zillij: Art of Moroccan Ceramics*. Garnet Publishing, Ltd 1992.

Darsh. S. M. *The Role of the Mosque in Islam.* Dar-us-Salam Publications. 1996

Deeb, Mary. J. Al Zaytuna; in *the Oxford Encyclopaedia of the Modern Islamic World*; vol. 4 ed. J. L. Esposito. New York: Oxford University Press; 1995.

Degeorge, Gerard and Porter, Yves. *The Art of the Islamic Tile*. Paris: Flammarion, 2002.

Djait, Hicham et al: *Histoire de la Tunisie* (Le Moyen Age). Tunis: Société Tunisienne de Diffusion. 1972

Dodge Bayard. *Muslim Education in the Medieval Times.* Washington D.C.: The Middle East Institute, 1962.

Eisner, Eliot W. *The Arts and the Creation of Mind.* New Haven: Yale University Press. 2005

Ettinghausen, Richard. Grabar, Oleg. Jenkins-Madina, Marilyn. *Islamic Art and Architecture. 650–1250*. Princeton and London: Yale University Press. 2001

Ettinghausen, Richard. "Islamic Carpets, The Joseph V McMullan Collection." *The Metropolitan Museum of Art Bulletin,* vol. 28 no. 10 (June 1970).

Encyclopaedia of Islam, new Edition, vol. 3. Leiden, Brill, 1971.

Frishman Martin and Khan, Hasan-Uddin eds. *The Mosque: History, Architectural Development and Regional Diversity.* New York: Thames & Hudson. 2002

Gardner, Howard. *Multiple Intelligences: New Horizons in Theory and Practice.* New York: Basic Books; Reprint edition. 2008

Ghazaleh, Pascale ed. *Held in Trust: Waqf in the Islamic World.* Cairo and New York: the American University in Cairo Press, 2011.

Gilles, Roland. *Piece from a Saf Rug with three Niches, Arab World Institute, Paris.* Paris: Somogy Editions d'art, 2014.

Grabar, Oleg. "The Mosque in Islamic Society Today". In: *The Mosque: History, Architectural Development and Regional Diversity.* London: Thames & Hudson. 2002

Hillenbrand, Robert. *Islamic Architecture: Form, Function, and Meaning.* New York: Columbia. University Press, 1994.

Hofmann, Murad. W. *Journey to Makkah*. Beltsville: Amana Publications. 1998

Inay, Ozlem and Erten, Oguz. *Turkish tiles. Turkey, Istanbul*. Istanbul: Silk Road Publications. 2013

Khoury, N. Nuha. "The Mihrab: From Text to Form," *International Journal of Middle East Studies*, vol. 30, 1998.

Landau, Rom. "The Karaouine at Fes," *The Muslim World* 48 (April 1958): 104–12.

Le Tourneau, Roger. *Fes in the age of the Merinids*, tr., from French by B. A. Clement. Norman: University of Oklahoma Press, 1961.

Fes avant le protectorat, 453–71. Casablanca, Societe Maroccaine de Librairie et d'Edition, 1947.

Makdisi, George: "Islamic Schools," *Dictionary of the Middle Ages*, vol. 11; Charles Scribners and Sons, 1988.

The Rise of Humanism in Classical Islam and the Christian West. Edinburgh, Edinburgh University Press, 1990.

Marcy, R. E. G. *Oriental Prayer Rugs.* Leigh-on-Sea: F. Lewis Publishers, 1971.

Maury, Charlotte. "Depictions of the Haramayn on Ottoman tiles; content and context." In: *The Hajj; Collected Essays,* edited by Venetia Porter and Liana Saif. London: The British Museum. 2013.

Michell, George. *Architecture of the Islamic World.* London and New York: Thames & Hudson. 1995

Nasr, Seyyed Hossein. *An Introduction to Islamic Cosmological Doctrines*. Albany: State University of New York Press, 1993.

Nasr, Seyyed Hossein. *The Need for a Sacred Science*. Albany: State University of New York Press, 1993.

Norhayati Kassim, Nora'shikin Abdullah, Zafrullah B. Mohd Taib, 2014, "Decoration in Praying Hall of Mosque: A review of current literature." *Procedia – Social and Behavioral Sciences* 153. (2014): 55–60.

O'Kane, Bernard. *The Treasures of Islamic Art in the Museums of Cairo.* Cairo: The American University of Cairo Press. 2006

Perkins, David N. *The Intelligent Eye: Learning to Think by Looking at Art*. Santa Monica: Getty Center for Education in the Arts. 1994

Rosenfeld, Boris and Adolf P. Youschkevitch "Geometry," in Roshdi Rashed, ed., *Encyclopedia of the History of Arabic Science, Vol. 2*, 447–94. New York, Routledge. 1996

Ruggles, Fairchild. *Islamic Art and Visual Culture: An Anthology of Sources.* Hoboken: Whiley-Blackwell. 2011.

Sahih, Muslim. Viewed in October 2019. Retrieved from: https://sunnah.com/muslim 2019

Saoud, Rabah. "Introduction to Muslim art". *Foundation for Science Technology and Civilization* (2004): 1–17.

Scott, S. P.: *History of the Moorish Empire in Europe*, (vol. 3) Philadelphia and London, J. B. Lippincott Company, 1904.

Sibai, Mohammad M. *Mosque Libraries, an historical Study*. London and New York: Mansell Publishing Ltd. 1987.

Singer, Amy. *Constructing Ottoman Beneficence. An Imperial Soup Kitchen in Jerusalem*. Albany: Suny Press. 2002

Singer, Lynette, eds. *The Minbar of Saladin: Reconstructing a Jewel of Islamic Art.* New York: Thames & Hudson. 2008

Sutton, Daud. *Islamic Design: A Genius for Geometry*. Glastonbury: Wooden Books. 2007.

Stanly, Tim. Palace and Mosque. Islamic Art from the Middle East. London: Victoria and Albert Museum. 2004.

Stetkevych, Jaroslav. *The Zephyrs of Najd: The Poetics of Nostalgia in the Classical Arabic Nasib*. Chicago and London: University of Chicago Press. 1993

Stierlin, Henri. *Islam: from Baghdad to Cordoba.* Cologne: Taschen. 2009

Tibawi, Abdul Latif. *Islamic Education*. London, Luzac and Company Ltd. 1972.

Totah, Khalil. *The Contribution of the Arabs to Education*. New York: Columbia University, 1926.

Tritton, Arthur Stanley. *Materials on Muslim education in the Middle Ages*. London, Luzac and Company. 1957

Ulrich, Marzolph. "From Mecca to Mashhad: The narrative of an illustrated Shi'i pilgrimage scroll from the Qajar period." Muqarnas Online 31(1) (2014): 207–42.

Wakfiyya Al Ghuriyya. Record 882. Cairo, Egyptian Ministry of Endowments, 1503.

Williams, Caroline, "The Cult of 'Alid Saints in the Fatimid Monuments of Cairo Part II: The Mausolea," *Muqarnas*, vol. 3 (1985).

Image Credits

Museum of Islamic Art, Cairo: 1.5, 1.6, 1.7, 1.9, 3.4, 3.5, 3.6, 3.7, 3.8, 3.9, 3.10, 3.12, 3.13, 3.14, 3.16, 3.17, 3.18, 3.19, 3.21, 3.22, 3.23, 4.1, 4.5, 4.6, 4.7, 4.8, 5.13, 5.14, 5.15, 5.16, 5.17, 5.18, 5.21, 5.24, 5.25, 5.28, 5.29, 6.19, 6.20, 6.21, 6.22, 6.23, 6.24, 6.25, 6.26, 6.27, 7.1, 7.5, 7.6, 7.7, 7.8, 7.9, 7.10, 7.11, 7.12, 7.13, 7.14, 7.15, 7.16, 7.17, 7.18, 8.1, 8.5, 8.6, 8.7, 8.8, 9.5, 9.6, 9.7, 9.8, 9.9. The Ministry of Tourism of Saudi Arabia: 1.9, 3.15, 3.24. Ithra: 1.1, 1.2, 1.8, 2.2, 3.1, 3.11, 3.20, 4.2, 4.3, 4.9, 5.4, 5.6, 5.7, 5.8, 5.9, 5.10, 5.11, 5.12, 5.19, 5.20, 5.22, 5.23, 5.26, 5.27, 6.1, 6.13, 6.14, 6.15, 6.16, 6.17, 6.18, 9.3, 10.5, 10.6. Sami Angawi (researcher), Mai Al-Naimi (Render), Eric Tang (3D model) 2.5, Raeda Ashour 4.4. Lisa Delong 6.2, 6.3, 6.4, 6.5, 6.6, 6.7, 6.8, 6.9, 6.10, 6.11, 6.12. Idries Trevathan 2.6. Abdullah Alkadi 1.3. www.agefotostock.com/ De Agostini Editore 8.4. Alamy Stock Photos: Eric Reisenberger 1.4, Alpha Stock 2.1, RM 2.3, Ramlan Bin Abdul Jalil 2.4, Granger Historical Picture Archive 2.7, 8.2, 10.2, Ahmad Faizal Yahya 2.8, Art Collection 2 3.2, Andrey Shevchenko 3.3, Images & Stories 5.1, Classic Image 5.2, Kevin Snelling 5.3, Hemis 5.5, Wael Hamdan 7.2, 7.3, Travelpixs 7.4, 10.4. ImageBROKER 8.3, Dimitar Chobanov 9.1, Dinosmichail 9.2, Dimitris Dimitris 9.4, World History Archive 10.1, Maor Winetrob 10.3, Robertharding 10.7, 10.8, Arthur Greenberg 10.9, B. O'Kane 10.10.

Colophon

This catalogue has been published in conjunction with the exhibition

Shatr AlMasjid: The Art of Orientation

organized by the King Abdulaziz Center for World Culture (Ithra) with works from the Museum of Islamic Art in Cairo (under the auspices of the Supreme Council of Egyptian Antiquities) and the National Museum in Riyadh (under the Ministry of Tourism of Saudi Arabia).

The exhibition is curated by
Idries Trevathan and Mona AlJalhami

Exhibition dates
January 2021 – October 2022

Published by:
Hirmer Publishers
Bayerstraße 57–59
80335 Munich
Germany
T. +49 (0)89 12 15 160
F. +49 (0)89 12 15 1610
www.hirmerpublishers.com

Edited and written by:
Idries Trevathan, Mona AlJalhami,
Murdo MacLeod, Mona Mansour

With contributions from:
Abdullah H. Alkadi, Sami Angawi,
Raeda Ashour, Lisa DeLong, Mohammed Abdel Bari, Oludamini Ogunnaike,
Mohamed Abd el-Salam, Minwer al-Meheid

English translation: Mohammad Shaban
English copyediting: Jane Robson
English proofreading: Danko Szabó
Design and project management:
Academic Publishing Service Gunnar Musan
Art direction: Mai Al-Naimi
Senior editor at Hirmer Publishers:
Elisabeth Rochau-Shalem
Additional project management
at Hirmer Publishers: Rainer Arnold
Lithography and pre-press:
Reproline Genceller, Munich
Paper: Gardamatt Art 150 g/m²
Typeface: Calluna
Printer: Printer Trento s.r.l.
Printed in Italy

ISBN 978-3-7774-3593-0